A GUIDE FOR FIELD WORKERS IN FOLKLORE

by KENNETH S. GOLDSTEIN

Preface by HAMISH HENDERSON

FOLKLORE ASSOCIATES, INC.
HATBORO, PENNSYLVANIA
1964

LIBRARY OF CONGRESS CATALOG CARD NUMBER: 64-24801

Manufactured in the U.S.A.
by Towne Printing Inc., Hatboro, Pa.

For VANCE RANDOLPH

and

MACEDWARD LEACH

PREFACE

FOLKLORISTS are an individualistic crew. Like the battered swaddies of Fred Karno's army—or like "Slattery's Mounted Fut"—they come in all shapes and sizes and disguises. There are the prim, the potlucky, and the pixillated. There are "the long and the short and the tall."

Some collect, some use collections, some do both. And there is always, of course, a sizable floating reserve of those who haven't done either for quite a while. What makes them do what they do? And what exactly is it that they are supposed to be doing? Different answers have been ventured to these questions—almost as many, in fact, as there have been folklorists willing to venture them. And now and then one hears in the background the drier comments of psychologists, anthropologists, and social historians.

The conviction has been growing for years among professional folklorists that if folklore studies are to achieve full academic status, this reputation for bizarre waywardness and indiscipline must be liquidated. One of the many merits of Dr. Goldstein's thoughtful and thought-provoking book is that it makes no bones about where it stands on this issue; indeed, it is itself a powerful accession to the ranks of the New Model Army of scientific folklorism. Its explicit aim is to turn as many amateur folklorists as possible into professionals.

As a Scottish collector who owes a very great deal to American encouragement and practical support, I am exceedingly glad to be able to recommend an American scholar's work to the attention of all fellow folklorists. A large part of what I myself know about folklore collecting I learned from Alan Lomax in the summer of 1951, and with every year that goes by I become more and more conscious of how much Europe owes to the great achievements of American scholarship in this field.

Dr. Goldstein has done Scotland several good services. He spent a year in Aberdeenshire not long back, and did some first-rate collecting there under the aegis of the School of Scottish Studies of Edinburgh University. After his return to the States in 1960, he reprinted, in the course of his activities as a publisher, a number of Scottish folk-song classics: the *Orpheus Caledonius* of William Thomson, James Johnson's *Scots Musical Museum*, James C. Dick's *Song of Robert Burns* and Gavin Greig's *Folk-Song of the North-East*. And as a result of his collecting experiences in Scotland as well as in the United States, he has written this most useful *Guide*—a pioneer attempt to work out a comprehensive methodology for field workers in folklore.

It goes without saying that in an ambitious work of this kind there are bound to be passages which will not please everyone—and maybe a few which will provoke lively disagreement. It is therefore perhaps just as well for me to stress here what Dr. Goldstein himself says in his first chapter, that "a methodology is only one of the requirements for successful collecting." I am sure that no collector, experienced or inexperienced, can fail to profit from a careful study of this book, but its author would be

the first to agree that a little experience gained in the field
is likely to be more important for the collector than even
the most stimulating and suggestive book theory. An
apprentice collector who thinks he can use this *Guide* as a
sort of "Do It Yourself" *vade mecum,* without taking the
trouble to assimilate it, will find that he is walking on
stilts over the landscape, instead of on shank's pony.

There are two points I'd like to make. The first is about
the place in the scheme of things of the resident collector.
Dr. Goldstein writes: "Anyone is capable of doing a certain amount of collecting, though not in 'the field'." It
seems to me there is a real and vital distinction to be made
between the collector who enters a community from the
outside—whether it is from another county or from another
continent—and the collector who is, so to speak, part and
parcel of the landscape of his own community. The
resident collector (Gavin Greig is a superb example) cannot properly be viewed as an accident in tradition. He is
in many ways an integral *part* of tradition, a chronicler
and remembrancer of the culture around him; he has no
need to assume a role because his role is obvious for all to
see. With any luck, he may actually preserve and foster
as much culture as he puts on record.

The second point is about the incoming collector who
does not make himself conspicuous. My experience is that
there is a kind of collector who can remain, by accident or
by design, almost as "invisible" as the postman in one of
G. K. Chesterton's "Father Brown" stories. The "quiet
man" collector of this sort who eschews a conspicuous
posture may in certain situations be well equipped to
solve a particular folklore problem.

There are, in fact, as hardly needs saying, many different kinds of collectors, and each will naturally make use
of his own personal advantages and abilities. However, I
fancy that most successful collectors do, in fact, have
something in common. Dr. Goldstein comes near the heart

of the matter when he says, commenting on a remark by
Samuel P. Bayard: "The collector who is incapable of
becoming involved with his informants, of developing a
'deep loving regard' for them, had best restrict his collecting to 'transient' folklore."

The collector-folklorist should never, in the heat of the
chase, forget his humanist role. He is helping to interpret
man to man—his beliefs, glories, dreams, darknesses. If he
adopts a patronizing attitude to what he is studying, he
may well blind himself to its real nature. And if he treats
his informants purely as sources of information, to be
taken up and discarded as occasion demands, he is in grave
danger of losing more than their friendship. A friend of
mine wrote recently: "My feeling is that, if one has a
normal degree of sensitivity, personal relations with singers
and musicians become so close that one soon reaches the
point at which it is impossible to accommodate any new
friendships."

Although every collector must size up for himself his
own position and the demands of his task at any given
time, he can never afford to leave such reflections as these
out of his calculations. If ever an academic collector is
tempted to proceed on the assumption that he "knows"
more about folklore than his informants do, he'd be well
advised to remember the wise words of A. N. Whitehead:
"The self-confidence of learned people is the comic tragedy
of civilization."

I hope Dr. Goldstein's Guide will be widely used, and
that it will encourage many people interested in folk
traditions to become collectors. In the nature of things
it won't be possible for more than a very few of these
recruits to folklore collecting to embark on full scale field
work. However, the evening or "Sunday" collector can take
comfort in the fact that much of the best collecting of the
past has been done precisely by the part-time amateur—
especially if he knows his own area well and has a real

sympathy with its traditions. All such collectors, and not only the lucky "full-timers," will find Dr. Goldstein's *Guide* an exceedingly useful work of reference.

HAMISH HENDERSON

School of Scottish Studies
Edinburgh University

FOREWORD

THE METHODS described in this *Guide* have grown out of
my early groping as a self-trained folklorist seeking collecting methods that would satisfactorily supply the answers
to certain field problems as I saw them at the time. From
this groping stage, I developed a curiosity about field work
techniques, and began to read available literature
on the methods of field workers in folklore, cultural
anthropology, sociology, psychology, and social work. In
folklore and anthropology, the methods were rarely described, and then only in the most general terms, as if the
methods were so well established and widely employed that
no discussion of them was really needed. The fields of
psychology, sociology, and social work offered considerable
material, some of it exceedingly helpful in the areas of observational and interviewing techniques, but the greatest
portion of it involved excessively (to me) detailed and
highly specialized knowledge in the respective fields.

An attempted synthesis of the methods suggested by
my reading pointed increasingly to the fact that folklore
as a discipline had few systematized field methods of its
own, and that the methods of cultural anthropologists

(some of whom had done much work in collecting folklore materials and data) were closest to satisfying the needs of field workers in folklore. However, the methods of anthropological folklorists were certainly not of the order which would permit simply borrowing them *en masse*. The anthropological folklorist was more anthropologist than folklorist; when he collected folklore, it was to serve the needs of anthropological theory and problem solving. It became apparent to me that what was needed was an effort at evolving methods, borrowing heavily from ethnography, and developing new approaches or refining existing ones to serve the ends of folklore in terms of folklore theory and problem solving.

Between 1951 and 1957 I spent every summer on field trips in upstate New York (1951), eastern Massachusetts (1955), and western North Carolina (1952, 1953, 1954, 1956, 1957), testing methods described or implied in my readings, modifying or improving them where necessary, and working out new methods where my field work suggested them. Sometimes my informants would make casual remarks or give information which would suggest another tack or approach to be defined and then tested. Often a collecting device or technique was conceived on the spur of the moment. If it proved successful, I rationalized what I had done and repeated it on appropriate occasions until I was able to ascertain its value as a technique to be applied generally in later field work.

During the nine or ten months of the year when the necessity of earning a living kept me out of field work, I continued reading in folklore and anthropology. As new books and articles were published, I found that increased attention was being paid to field methods and that some of my field experiments coincided with already established procedures and methods. Especially rewarding in this regard were the articles and bibliographies on "Problems of Process" in *Anthropology Today*, edited by A. L.

Kroeber (Chicago, 1953), pages 401-487, and the discussions of these papers in *An Appraisal of Anthropology Today* (Chicago, 1953), pages 85-103. Other details discussed in these works suggested further approaches to be tried during the following summer's field work.

Perhaps the most important single conviction which developed from these readings and from my increasing contacts with professional folklorists through the agency of American Folklore Society meetings and correspondence was that I should pass beyond the stage of a self-trained amateur and seek academic training in folklore. In 1957 I attended classes at Columbia University on anthropological community studies and the history of anthropology. Stimulated by these courses, I decided to continue my studies, this time towards a graduate degree, at some university where I could obtain training in both folklore and anthropology (Columbia offered no folklore courses at that time). After being accepted at the University of Pennsylvania as a graduate student, I enrolled at the Folklore Institute of Indiana University for the summer of 1958, there studying to good advantage under Archer Taylor, Warren Roberts, and W. Edson Richmond, as well as basking in the intense heat of folklore inspiration from numerous other attendant scholars and students at the Institute. Taking up my course work at the University of Pennsylvania, my training in folklore and cultural anthropology under MacEdward Leach, Tristram P. Coffin, A. Irving Hallowell, and Ward Goodenough helped to crystallize concepts applicable to my developing field methodology as well as supplying new ideas to be tested on some future field trip. Thus stimulated, I applied for a United States government grant under the Fulbright Act to do field work in Scotland, where I could test field methods under conditions different from those in which they were conceived. My plan was to

. . . study the collecting techniques of the leading
Scottish field workers, and by applying to these
techniques the methodology developed in field work
in parts of New England and the Southern Appalachians . . . to collect a representative sampling of the
folklore and folklore traditions of a typical Scots
Lowland community. . . . By relating these traditions
to other aspects of community life . . . to indicate
their importance to the cultural complex of that
community. (Quotation from my *Statement of
Plans for Research* submitted during November, 1958,
in my application for appointment as a Fulbright
Scholar in the United Kingdom.)

I was awarded the grant, and in September of 1959 I
arrived in Britain, did some research in London, and then
went on to Scotland, where I spent three weeks at the
School of Scottish Studies preparing myself for fieldwork
under the direction of Hamish Henderson, Scotland's
leading collector of Lowland Scots traditions.

In October of that year I began field work in the Buchan
District of Aberdeenshire, traditionally the most vital
folklore area in all of Lowland Scotland. During the next
ten months I was able to apply to the field conditions at
hand most of the techniques and methods which I had
worked out in the United States. In the course of my work
I refined these methods still further. After my return to
the United States in the fall of 1960, I was able to evaluate
my methods and by deduction to refine them still further.
Continued course work at the University of Pennsylvania
helped to set my findings in perspective, leading to the
present work which in its original form served as my doc-
toral dissertation.

This book, therefore, is the result of an attempt to
establish a methodology for field workers in folkore. The
success of its application may depend upon how conscien-

tiously a collector follows its suggestions. It can serve still
more importantly, however, to encourage further experi-
mentation along lines similar to those suggested above.
The present work is far from a final statement; indeed,
there can be no final statement. It is rather a preliminary
report. Present chapters will have to be rewritten and
new chapters added by the people to whom this work is
directed—present and future folklore collectors.

* * *

I wish to acknowldge help in the preparation of this
work given to me by my friends and colleagues in folklore.
First, there are those with whom I spent delightful hours
of conversation about collecting folklore at a time when
my own ideas were still forming. I have no doubt I
appropriated some of their concepts. In the course of their
reading this *Guide,* if they recognize certain ideas as being
unmistakably theirs, I hope they will forgive me for the
seemingly silent appropriation I have made of those ideas.
In this respect I wish especially to thank Vance Randolph,
MacEdward Leach, Herbert Halpert, Harry Oster, Hamish
Henderson, A. L. Lloyd, Frank Hoffmann, Ellen Stekert,
Bruce Buckley, Alan Lomax, Edith Fowke, and Ed Cray.

Next, there are those people, both friends and strangers,
whose writings have contributed heavily to the shaping of
my ideas. Their names will be found in appropriate places
throughout the text or in the footnotes of this work. If I
do not mention them by name at this point it is merely
because there are so many who have been helpful in this
manner.

To my friends who were also my teachers I am grateful
on many accounts—for their encouragement, supervision,
criticism, and final approval of the dissertation on which
this book is based. Here I must especially thank Mac-
Edward Leach, Tristram P. Coffin, and Ward Goodenough.

Copies of this work in typescript form were sent to several folklorists for their comments and criticism. Charles Seeger, D. K. Wilgus, Samuel P. Bayard, and Roger D. Abrahams proved by their general lack of disagreement with what I had to say that they were very good, but bashful, friends. I hope they will have the opportunity to review this work for some journal. I hasten to assure them that their critical comments after the fact of publication will in no way strain our relationships.

Hamish Henderson, Alan Lomax, and Herbert Halpert also proved to be good friends, not only to me but to all folklorists, by supplying the criticism which I sought. I am grateful to them for the considerable time and care with which they examined the manuscript and for their cogent and incisive commentaries. Where I accepted their criticism and suggestions and made the appropriate changes, additions or emendations, the present work can not be faulted. The final reading was made by John Greenway, editor of the Memoirs of the American Folklore Society (in which series this work is included), and I am grateful to him for the valuable criticism which he gave relative to content, style, and copy editing.

Of the many things for which I am grateful to my wife, Rochelle, and to my children, Rhoda, Diane, Karl and Scott, not the least is the good humor with which they put up with the irascibility to which I subjected them during the periods in which this work was written and revised.

KENNETH S. GOLDSTEIN

University of Pennsylvania
Philadelphia, Pennsylvania
May, 1964

CONTENTS

Preface vii

Foreword xiii

I. Introduction 1

II. Problem Statement and Analysis 13

III. Time Considerations 27

IV. Pre-Field Preparations 36

V. Rapport Establishment and Maintenance . . 47

VI. Observation Collecting Methods 77

VII. Interview Collecting Methods 104

VIII. Supplementary Field Methods 144

IX. Motivation and Remuneration of Informants . 160

Afterword 175

Bibliography 177

Index 189

CHAPTER I

Introduction

THE BASIS OF ANY SCHOLARLY DISCIPLINE is the materials with which it deals. Without such materials there can be no subject for scholarship. For the historian these materials consist of historical data, for the literary scholar they consist of literature, for the folklorist they consist of the materials which he calls folklore.

There may be little agreement among the members of the discipline as to which materials fall properly within the domain of their study. In the case of folklore this may appear to be a very acute problem, as the twenty-one definitions of folklore to be found in the *Standard Dictionary*[1] attest; but despite such variance of opinion there

1. *Funk & Wagnalls Standard Dictionary of Folklore Mythology and Legend*, eds. Maria Leach and Jerome Fried (New York, 1949), Vol. I, pp. 398-403. Apart from this reference and footnotes 9 and 29 in this chapter, I see no point in getting involved further in the problem of definitions. Enough, perhaps too much, already has been written on the subject and folklorists are still no closer to agreement than they were when the term folklore was first coined in 1846. Interestingly enough, though they rarely agree, they also rarely have any difficulty in comprehending each other.

1

is a certain core of materials which all definitions recognize as belonging to folklore.[2]

Just as there is no one definition of folklore, there is no one approach to folklore studies. One scholar has described at least seven varieties of the species recognized as folklorists,[3] and others can probably be added to that list.[4] The only truly common ground that all of these share is that they are concerned in some way with the materials of folklore.

The evaluation, interpretation, and analysis of these materials will follow from the various approaches, which in turn are determined, at least in part, by the definitions. Whether such evaluation, interpretation, or analysis is basically humanistic or social-scientific (or a combination of these) will depend upon the training, the predilections of the persons involved, and the scholarly apparatus utilized by the handlers of these materials. Here again, nearly the only thing common to all these persons will be the materials with which they are working. It should be obvious from this delineation that any approach to the field of folklore must begin with the materials of folklore.

These materials can come only from the collector of folklore—using the term "collector" in the broadest sense possible. He is the most important element in the scholarship of folklore, as even the non-collector readily admits.[5]

2. Stith Thompson, "Advances in Folklore Studies" in *Anthropology Today*, ed. A. L. Kroeber (Chicago, 1953), p. 588.

3. Richard M. Dorson, "A Theory for American Folklore," *JAF* 72 (1959), pp. 197-202. Dorson classifies the seven types as (1) comparative folklorists, (2) cultural anthropologists, (3) folksong and folkmusic specialists, (4) special pleaders, (5) regional collectors, (6) literary historians, and (7) popularizers.

4. For example, literary aestheticians (not to be confused with literary historians), folk religionists, and applied folklorists (those utilizing folklore for creating understanding between groups, not to be confused with Dorson's category seven, "popularizers"), come most readily to mind.

5. Alexander H. Krappe, "The Comparative Approach in Europe" in "Conference on the Character and State of Studies in Folklore," *JAF* 59 (1946), p. 500, states:

. . . there is a certain contrast brought out between field workers and library or laboratory workers . . . The field worker is

The collector may be a professional folklorist[6] or an amateur.[7] He may have consciously sought out such materials with an awareness of what they are, or he may have no idea that they belong to a category of cultural materials termed folklore. His materials may be published as folklore collectanea or be included (by him or others) in non-folkloristic works, such as histories, diaries, newspaper articles, travel books, or literary works. But in every case, his materials will be evaluated as to their authenticity, accuracy, and degree of details and general reliability before they are used by folklore scholars.

Sources considered unreliable may still supply a scholar with an indication of where, when, and with whom some item of folklore existed. A scholar making a study of a tale by means of the historic-geographic method may use such information for placing a tale version within the scheme of his analysis, but he is unlikely to use the tale itself for any but the most tentative of conclusions. For a study of the changes which have taken place in the specific content of the tale, the comparative folklorist will use only those versions which he considers reliable as to such content. For such an analysis, a mere outline of the tale's elements may be sufficient, containing only an indication of its motifs and traits. The literary aesthetician will not be content with such an outline; he will demand the complete tale as told by the teller. Only from this can he make his aesthetic evaluations. The social scientist (cultural

undoubtedly doing the more important work (I can say this because I have never been a field worker and never expect to be one), because without him the analyst would have nothing to do.

6. For the purpose of this present work I define professional folklorists as those who have been academically trained in folklore studies and who devote a considerable part of their energy to the study of folklore.

7. M. A. Murray's definition of an amateur as "the self-trained" folklorist, rather than an untrained enthusiast, is an excellent one, and the term "amateur" will be used in that sense throughout this work. See M. A. Murray, "England as a Field for Folklore Research," *Folklore* 65 (1954), p. 8.

4 A GUIDE FOR FIELD WORKERS IN FOLKLORE

anthropologist, sociologist, or psychologist) will demand
still more. Not only does he want an accurately transcribed
text, but he will insist that its transcription be ac-
companied by a full description of the milieu in which it
was collected, the mannerisms and gestures of the tale-
teller (the physical and psychological factors contributing
to his style) , the audience (its make-up, relationship to the
teller, and its reactions) , and the meaning which the tale
has for the members of the society. Some of this information may be obtained from the tale itself or from the
description of the milieu; other information may have
to be obtained from interviews.

Many folklorists belong to no one school and range
widely in their use of available methods. A literary
aesthetician, for example, concerned with the folktale as
oral literature, will interest himself not only in the
material, but in its matrix, in its bearers, and in their folk
aesthetic.[8] His needs are almost identical with those of
the anthropological folklorist. The two may analyze their
materials differently, but the nature and reliability of
their basic data are of almost the same order.

In short, every approach extracts from the given data the
information it needs to accomplish its ends. The work of
an untrained observer or collector will supply some data
usable to all of the approaches mentioned, but will satisfy
none completely. The collector (amateur or professional)
who supplies only an outline of the text and data as to
where, when, and by whom it was narrated may satisfy the
comparative folklorist, but will not meet the needs of the
literary or anthropological folklorist. The collector who
takes down a word-for-word transcription of the text,
together with time and place data, may satisfy the comparative and literary folklorists, but has not fulfilled the needs
of the anthropologist. But the collector who supplies all of

8. For the ideal statement of such an approach see MacEdward Leach,
"Problems of Collecting Oral Literature," *PMLA* 77 (1962), pp. 335-340.

the data necessary to make the anthropologist happy also fulfills the needs of the comparative and literary folklorists. More than likely such data will also be sufficient for any other approach. It would appear from this that the methods of collecting which are to be most encouraged are those which will supply the greatest amount of reliable information to the largest number of potential users of such information.[9]

At the present time, however, there exists no handbook to guide collectors or instruct folklore students in the best methods and techniques of collecting. There are manuals for collecting specific genres of lore, such as folk music and dance,[10] but none give a comprehensive methodology. There are also several useful handbooks of folklore,[11] but they contain mainly a description of the kinds of materials which are folklore and detailed sets of questions to be used in soliciting information from informants. One of them contains only six pages of general instructions for collecting,[12] another contains fourteen pages,[13] and a

9. I do not mean to imply that the folklore collector is a kind of service man for other academicians who may find his materials pertinent to their own studies. The degree to which folklore materials provide a systematic view of the creative activities of mankind, serving as the main forms developed for expressing human emotion throughout history, as well as providing the principal sources for explicitly expressed goals, fantasies, and dreams—to that degree folklore is a prime source of data; in best serving the aims of folklore scholarship, the collector may also serve scholars in other fields. But altruism on the part of professional folklore field workers towards other disciplines should not obscure the fact that the work of these collectors is primarily designed to serve the aims and needs of folklore scholarship.

10. Maud Karpeles (ed.), *The Collecting of Folk Music and Other Ethnomusicological Material* (London, 1958), and Ljubica S. Yanković, *Instructions for Collecting Material Regarding Folk Dances* (Belgrade, 1940).

11. George L. Gomme, *The Handbook of Folklore* (London, 1890); C. S. Burne, *The Handbook of Folklore* (London, 1914), (revised and enlarged edition of the preceding title); Seán O Súilleabháin, *A Handbook of Irish Folklore* (Dublin, 1942), (a reprint edition with a new foreword by the author has been published by Folklore Associates, Hatboro, Pennsylvania, 1963).

12. Gomme, *Handbook*, Chapter XXII, "The Way to Collect Folklore," pp. 167-172.

13. Burne, *Handbook*, pp. 6-19.

third contains only three pages[14] of such instructions. While these handbooks will serve the collector well as questionnaires, they cannot be considered as adequately fulfilling the need for a methodology in folklore collecting.

We must turn to the cultural anthropologists for anything approaching an adequate methodology for folklore field workers. If cultural anthropology has moved past folklore in achieving status as an academic discipline, it is because of the realization by its workers that its methods must be scientifically determined and based.[15] If anthropologists frequently look upon folklorists as amateurs having a good time puttering around in the field of culture collecting, it is because folklorists have neither developed any systematic collecting methods of their own nor adequately employed the methods developed by anthropologists.[16]

14. Ó Súilleabháin, Handbook, "Instructions to Collectors," pp. xi-xiii.

15. This is not to say, however, that anthropology is presently to be considered a fully scientific discipline. Too much of its analysis is still dependent upon the talents of individual investigators rather than upon objective methods of data gathering.

16. There is yet another count of amateurism with which folklorists can be charged. They are also guilty of doing next to nothing with their materials after they have collected them. The preoccupation of folklorists with form and structure—which amounts to practically the only analysis they have attempted of the collected materials of folklore—has rarely been commented upon by critics of folklore scholarship. Gershon Legman, in The Horn Book (New Hyde Park, N. Y., 1964), more than makes up for this lack of criticism in a scathingly worded attack:

> The curse of folklore and folksong publication . . . has been this endless doodling with the unimportant and non-significant paraphernalia of form . . . without any matching concentration on meaning and function; with no study, until barely yesterday, of what the material means to the people who transmit it . . . ; what it tells us about their inner aspirations and their response to the lives they live. (p. 285)

and again:

> It is not enough . . . to publish raw collections of folk tales and folk materials . . What is necessary now, and long overdue, is to base publication deeply upon some meaningful and mature interpretation—socio-analytic, or psycho-analytic, or any other kind of analytic so long as it is analyzed—of what the material means, and meant to the people who have transmitted it. (p. 254)

There is no one method for field work in anthropology, just as there can be no one method for field work in folklore. But anthropologists have settled on a systematic approach to field work which may be termed a general methodology, within which various field workers may perfect their own techniques. Training in field methods, while continuing to be improved and sharpened, is "recognized as a necessary part of most university courses in anthropology."[17] It is essential for the future of folklore studies that similar training in folklore field work be instituted in university courses, undergraduate and graduate.[18]

The best of America's folklore collectors have for some time been aware of the ethnographic approach to field work. And they have usually been quite vocal in their efforts to interest other field workers in this approach. Herbert Halpert, trained in both anthropology and literature,[19] has frequently called upon non-anthropological folklorists to utilize the ethnographic approach.[20] Alan Lomax, the most wide-ranging of all our field workers, has stressed the value of a functional approach, using enthnographic methods.[21] MacEdward Leach, who is proud to call himself a literary folklorist, has instructed his students and fellow members of the Modern Language Association that "anthropologists have much to teach collectors of

17. Audrey I. Richards, "The Development of Field Work Methods in Social Anthropology," Chapter XII in *The Study of Society: Methods and Problems* (London, 1939), p. 274.

18. At present, I believe systematic training in folklore field work in America is available only at the University of California at Los Angeles, Indiana University, and the University of Pennsylvania.

19. Herbert Halpert, "Some Undeveloped Areas in American Folklore," *JAF* 70 (1957), p. 299.

20. See, for example, Halpert's articles: "American Regional Folklore" in "Folklore Research in North America," *JAF* 60 (1947), pp. 355-366, and "The Functional Approach" in "Conference on the Character and State of Studies in Folklore," *JAF* 59 (1946), pp. 510-512.

21. Alan Lomax, "The Functional Aspects of Folklore" in "Conference on the Character and State of Studies in Folklore," *JAF* 59 (1946), pp. 507-510.

8 A GUIDE FOR FIELD WORKERS IN FOLKLORE

folklore and oral literature."[22] And perhaps the most vocal
of the non-anthropological folklorists to deal with this
matter has been the historian-folklorist Richard Dorson,
who has reiterated that "fieldworkers could profit from
ethnographical studies."[23]

Anthropological folklorists have shown the way. From
Franz Boas, who early in this century developed methods
and standards for field work which still have relevance to
our problems,[24] through Melville Herskovits, William
Bascom, and many others, cultural anthropologists have
shown by their words but even more frequently by their
deeds the way to achieve success in the field.

To admit the value of anthropological techniques does
not, however, mean that we must slavishly follow the
various schools of anthropological theory. To borrow from
the ethnographic approach to field work does not imply
that we have to assume, for example, an extreme functionalist attitude. We are concerned with the traditions
of folklore, the materials, and the process, and we can
apply scientific standards to our field work in securing
information about them, but we need not apply any
holistic approach in which our interest in folklore forces
us to study all of culture in the unrealistic belief that "no
part of [it] is to be understood except in its relation to the
totality of which it is a part."[25]

22. MacEdward Leach, "Problems of Collecting Oral Literature," PMLA
77 (1962), p. 335.
23. Richard M. Dorson, "Standards for Collecting and Publishing
American Folktales" in "The Folktale: A Symposium," JAF 70 (1957),
p. 54.
24. For Boas' contributions to field work methods, see Robert H.
Lowie, The History of Ethnological Theory (New York, 1937), pp. 131-
136, and Melville Jacobs, "Folklore" in The Anthropology of Franz Boas
(San Francisco, 1959), pp. 119-123.
25. Quotation from Melville Herskovits describing a functionalist approach in "Some Problems of Method in Ethnography" in Method and
Perspective in Anthropology, ed. Robert F. Spencer (Minneapolis, 1954),
p. 3.

In line with the above remarks, this book presents an essentially ethnographic approach to folklore field work, conceived in terms of the needs and problems of modern folklore concepts and theory.

* * *

There are certain limitations and stipulations which must be placed on the use of this methodology, deriving from the nature of folklore field work and from the manner in which the present methodology was evolved.

This book cannot make a folklorist a collector. A methodology is only one of the requirements for successful collecting. More important is the individual who would become a collector. If he does not have the inclination, temperament, or personality for collecting, he will not become a successful field worker merely by using the methods and techniques given here. While it is true that his inclinations can be changed by inspired instruction, temperament and personality go so much deeper that it is unlikely that they could be sufficiently affected. Still, anyone is capable of doing a certain amount of collecting, though not in "the field."[26] One can collect from family, friends, and neighbors, and to such collectors the basic requirements for obtaining data will apply as much as they do to qualified field workers.

Those who would use this *Guide* are expected to have a sufficient knowledge of the essentials of folklore (that is, knowledge of genres and certain basic folklore theory), which cannot and should not be part of a guide to collecting techniques and methods. This is not a "handbook" of folklore. The present work can be effectively used by both amateur (self-trained) and professional (academically-

26. By *field* collecting I mean that work which is done over a period of time by a collector living among his informants at a distance from his own home or country, and during which time his total energy and activity is directed at obtaining folklore materials and data from those informants.

trained) collectors, as long as they have sufficiently
prepared themselves in knowing what folklore consists of.
The present work involves field methods and techniques,
but is not in itself a questionnaire. For the specific questions to which the collector should obtain answers in the
course of his field work, the reader may utilize the O
Súilleabháin, Gomme, and Burne "Handbooks" and the
various questionnaires prepared by several European
archives,[27] as well as similar materials issued by regional
folklore societies.[28]

This *Guide* is based on collecting experiences and experiments conducted in "folk" communities, *i.e.*, essentially
rural, agriculturally-based, non-industrial communities,[29]
which traditionally have been the areas in which folklorists
have done most of their collecting. I cannot guarantee
the success of its application in non-folk, aboriginal, non-
or pre-literate areas of the world. Such areas have been
almost exclusively the domain of cultural anthropologists.
Anthropological collectors will utilize their own well-
established ethnographic methods. Since the present
methods have been based so largely on ethnographic

27. For details concerning the use of questionnaires in Europe, see
sections on "The Collecting of Folklore" and "The Archiving of Folklore" in *Four Symposia on Folklore*, ed. Stith Thompson (Bloomington,
1953), and E. J. Lindgren, "The Collection and Analysis of Folk-Lore,"
in *The Study of Society: Methods and Problems* (London, 1939), pp.
373-374.

28. See for example, S. J. Sackett and Wm. E. Koch, *An Instructional
Manual for Members of the Kansas Folklore Society* (Hays, Kansas, 1958).
For an earlier use of such questionnaires in America, see the excellent
one on folksongs prepared by Herbert Halpert in consultation with
George Herzog for the Joint Committee on Folk Arts, W.P.A. (n. p., 1939).

29. A proper definition of the folk is one which is not restricted to
rural peoples (among whom I have conducted the major portion of
my own field work) but which recognizes the existence of folk communities within urban and industrial centers. An excellent definition is given
by John Greenway, who views the folk as "an unsophisticated, homogeneous group living in a politically-bounded advanced culture but
isolated from it by such factors as topography, geography, religion, dialect, economics, and race." (*Literature Among the Primitives*, (Hatboro,
Pa., 1964), p. xii.

methods, I believe the non-anthropological folklorist could utilize the methods given here to good effect in areas usually covered by anthropologists, but I have not so tested these methods.

The present methodology has been worked out for the purpose of collecting specifically that "certain core of materials which all definitions recognize as belonging to folklore." I am not certain of its full applicability to the problems of collecting folk arts, crafts, and material culture. I believe that most of its methods will apply to a certain extent, but these will have to be supplemented by additional methods already devised successfully by enthnography and folk-life collectors in Europe. Those wishing to collect elements of material culture would do well to check with folk museums, which have, through specialization and concerted efforts, made adequate methods for such collection.

The methods in this book have been constucted mainly in terms of the individual collector working solo or at most in tandem with his wife and children. Team collecting must develop its own methods of cooperation and area delineation, though the methods suggested here will assist the individual members who make up such a team.

The present work does not include methods requiring special training and techniques, such as psychological or projective tests designed to obtain information about personality functioning. When a revised edition of this book is made, it should include one or more chapters on such techniques by persons properly qualified to instruct in them.

Finally, this methodology assumes the collector's full knowledge of his informant's language. While certain observation techniques can be reasonably well carried out by a collector unfamiliar with the language of the group

from whom collecting is being done, conversation, interviewing, and everyday socializing with key informants can
not, even with the aid of multilingual translators.

CHAPTER II

Problem Statement
and Analysis

THE PREPARATION OF A GUIDE for folklore field work
implies a concern with the status of the discipline of
folklore. It is part of a larger effort to raise the discipline
to the level of a science (a social science retaining close ties
with the humanities, to be sure).[1] Accordingly, these
methods should be considered within their conceptual
folkloristic framework.

This conceptual framework derives from the preliminary training in theory which the folklorist should
have for effective research either in the field or the library.
This training will enable him to prosecute a systematic
line of inquiry, to recognize what is relevant, and to make
judgments at critical points in his work. Such training
should also teach him to avoid bias in the observation and
recording of data, and to treat these data as facts which are
independent of any school of thought, theory, or approach.
It will also supply him with a conceptual scheme to determine not only the direction of his field work, but the
manner in which it is formulated as well.

1. See, for example, Herbert Halpert's remarks in "American Regional
Folklore," *JAF* 60 (1947), p. 361.

Much has been made of the fact that so much field work has been done by amateur collectors,[2] and that factors of personality frequently enable the amateur to do a job which few professional folklorists could do as well.[3] But it is not sufficient merely to recognize such a situation without doing something about it. As many of these amateurs as possible should be encouraged to become professionals. It is precisely because so much of the work in the past was done by amateurs that there exist huge collections of folklore, but collections without sufficient documentation and data about the processes of folklore and other problems of increasing interest to professional folklorists. Such documentation, which is essential if folklore is to achieve scientific status, can be supplied only by trained professional folklorists guided by a body of theory, or by amateurs trained by such professionals.

Every student of folklore should be trained as broadly as possible to enable him to make his own choice as to which approach or combination of approaches most satisfy him, and there should be no carping about the alleged superiority of one school of thought over any other. Each theoretical approach supplies the answers to its own problems as it defines them. When, for example, a field worker collects folklore for no purpose other than to describe what exists, it may appear to have been done without any explicit theory involved. Yet such a project could certainly have been undertaken within the theoretical framework of literary folklorists concerned only with the materials of folklore, and thereby represents the results

2. Stith Thompson, "American Folklore After Fifty Years," *JAF* 51 (1938), p. 2.

3. Charles Seeger, "Professionalism and Amateurism in the Study of Folk Music," *JAF* 62 (1949), pp. 107-13 (Reprinted in *The Critics and the Ballad*, ed. by MacEdward Leach and Tristram P. Coffin [Carbondale, Illinois, 1961], pp. 151-160.)

of systematic research.[4] At the opposite pole are those extreme functionalist-folklorists whose theoretical position maintains that no item of folklore may be understood without reference to the cultural whole of which it is a part; such collectors will obtain a full range of data by many methods.[5] The validity of either of these approaches is beside the point. What is significant is that though the methods and the kinds of materials collected differ the differences were traceable to the body of theory which inspired the collector. Both types of collector started with problems framed in terms of their respective schools of thought, and both obtained the data considered relative to the solution of those problems. "Theory is sometimes condemned by the unenlightened as involving 'preconceived ideas.' It involves rather preconceived problems."[6]

1. Scientific Inquiry

The conceptual framework of the folklorist will concern him for far longer time than that which he will actually spend in the field. It assists him in every stage of planning his field work as well. If he has been properly trained,

4. Much collecting in America has been executed or supervised by literary folklorists, the resulting collections when published frequently consisting mainly of the texts with literary headnote references to other texts.

5. This type of approach was carried out by Bronislaw Malinowski in his studies in the Trobriand Islands (see the chapter on mythology in *Argonauts of the Western Pacific* [London, 1922]) and applied by other anthropologists influenced by him. For an ideal statement of the functionalist approach to folklore, see Malinowski's *Myth in Primitive Psychology* (New York, 1926) where he states:

> Our conclusions imply a new method of treating the science of folk-lore, for we have shown that it cannot be independent of ritual, of sociology, or even of material culture. Folk-tales, legends, and myths must be lifted from their flat existence on paper, and placed in the three-dimensional reality of full-life. (p. 92)

6. Ralph Piddington, *An Introduction to Social Anthropology*, Vol. 2 (Edinburgh, 1957), p. 529.

including instruction in the logic of scientific inquiry,[7] he will know that the methods to be applied in the field constitute not an initial stage of inquiry but a later phase. Scientific inquiry involves the following stages:

1. *Problem statement*: the setting up of a problem to be solved.

2. *Analysis of the problem*: the determination of the relevant data and the methods most appropriate for obtaining them.

3. *The collection of data.*

4. *Presentation of the research findings.*

5. *Postulation of hypotheses, based on the analysis and interpretation of the data.*

Not all inquiry will proceed to the final stage. Where the problem is one of description, stage four will represent the end product. Where research has been undertaken to obtain data for the purpose of establishing an hypothesis, the fifth stage will be followed by beginning with the first stage again in terms of a new problem to test the hypothesis for the purpose of establishing laws.

The present work confines itself to the first three stages of inquiry; the first two stages to be discussed in this chapter and the third stage to constitute the bulk of the book.

2. Problem Statement

The initial stage of inquiry, problem statement, can not be sloughed off arbitrarily if we are to treat folklore as a science. Usually little attention is paid by the folklore collector to determining what problem is expected to be solved by field work. This is often the case with amateur

7. Such instruction can be readily obtained in F. S. C. Northrop, *The Logic of the Sciences and the Humanities* (New York, 1959).

collectors or those who spend their vacations (as vacations) in the field. Collecting for them is a pleasurable pursuit. The fact that the materials collected may later be useful to themselves or others remains at best a secondary consideration. Part of the reason for this may be that frequently "the most difficult portion of any inquiry is its initiation."[8] The vacation collector may not wish to burden himself with a displeasing task. The trained folklorist, devoted to his discipline, cannot indulge himself in this manner. All stages of the inquiry must be pursued with equal vigor. A collector may apply the most rigorous methods during the later stages of investigation, but if the problem itself has been superficially defined, the most scientific of methods may not retrieve the situation later on.

It is like a ship leaving port for a distant destination; a very slight erroneous deviation in taking one's bearing at the beginning may result in entirely missing one's mark at the end regardless of the sturdiness of one's craft or the excellence of one's subsequent seamanship.[9]

Collecting initiated without careful problem statement is usually arbitrary, unorganized, perfunctory, and wasteful. The time a collector spends in the field is rarely long enough even without such waste.

Without training in theory it is very unlikely that the collector will have any idea of what problems need solving. The theory of folklore which treated the materials as survivals[10] resulted in the collection of great masses of materials removed from their context and catalogued for the purposes of comparison and identification. Similarly,

8. Northrop, p. 1.
9. Northrop, p. 1.
10. See G. L. Gomme's *The Handbook of Folklore* (London, 1890), p. 5, where he gives the definition of "the Science of Folk-Lore" as " . . . *the comparison and identification of the survivals of archiac beliefs, customs, and traditions in modern ages.*"

a theory of folklore which treats the materials as oral art forms will result in the statement of problems leading to the collection of the materials in their fullest social and physical context.[11] Both these illustrations indicate exactly how theory-bound the problems of folklore can be.

Many field problems involve simply discovering and recording the traditions which exist among the folk of a specific region or area. MacEdward Leach's collecting project in Labrador in 1960 had as its purpose describing the folklore of a previously uncharted territory. Much of the early folksong collecting in the southern Appalachians and in New England served the same purpose. And there are still regions where similar projects may be carried out (for example, in North America, in the Rocky Mountain states and in the plains provinces of Canada.)

Closely related to such problems are those in which a collector chooses to re-survey an area in which no collecting has been done for some time and in which he hopes to discover what changes have taken place in the interim.

In either of these problem orientations—discovering traditions in uncharted regions, and resurveying regions in which collecting has previously been done—the collector may either stop at reporting what he has found, or he may go on to formulate hypotheses based on the materials or conditions which he has discovered. Should he proceed to the hypothesis-formulation stage, he has two steps open to him. He may either rest with his hypothesis and do nothing about proving his case (leaving it to others to do so), or he may return to the field to obtain the evidence to test his hypothesis. In the latter case, he begins anew with a problem stated in terms of his specific hypothesis.

In some cases a collector may start with the hypothesis-formulation stage on the basis of his readings and prior

11. MacEdward Leach, "Problems of Collecting Oral Literature," *PMLA* 77 (1962), pp. 335-340.

knowledge of the specific traditions or conditions in the region. The problem is stated in terms of an hypothesis and the collector proceeds into the field to discover data or materials which will either support or refute his theory. Richard Dorson has suggested that the American folklorist, like the anthropologist, should "base his field expeditions on an hypothesis and test it in the field with tough empirical data."[12] The suggestion is one which should be welcomed by all folklorists, not only by anthropologically oriented ones. Anthropologists, however, know how to test their hypotheses scientifically; until and unless non-anthropological folklorists receive training in the logic of science, the invitation to state field problems in terms of hypotheses may lead to faulty field methods and false conclusions. Consciously or unconsciously, a collector may shape his field materials to a specific predetermined conclusion intended to prove his hypothesis. MacEdward Leach cites an example in which:

> "a collection of folklore was made in Brittany some time ago to determine if Breton folklore was derived from Island Cymric. The collector, who was sure that it was, was inclined to suppress elements that tended to prove otherwise. And I am certain that it was unconscious on his part."[13]

In this case, we must assume that the collector's problem was improperly stated (if it was stated verbally at all). Based on his hypothesis, we might reconstruct his faulty problem statement like this: "To collect data to prove that Breton folklore is derived from Island Cymric." The error should be fairly obvious; his problem statement

12. Richard M. Dorson, "A Theory for American Folklore," *JAF* 72 (1959), p. 201.
13. Statement made by MacEdward Leach in an unpublished paper read at the First Intra-American Conference on Ethnomusicology, Cartagena, Columbia, February 27, 1963.

should have read: "To collect all data pertinent to the hypothesis in order to determine whether Breton folklore is derived from Island Cymric." Objectively collected, non-selected data, analyzed after the collector has returned from the field, should indicate the validity of his hypothesis.

3. Problem Analysis

The collector cannot simply proceed from the statement of the problem to collecting itself. To do so could result in as great a waste of time and energy as would an arbitrary treatment of the problem statement.

Since investigation begins with the statement of the problem, it is the problem which must lead us to the methods to be used in its solution. This is achieved through an analysis of the problem. Indeed, the analysis of the problem is so closely related to its statement that the two stages perhaps ought not to be considered separately and might well be merged into one.[14]

It is the aim of the analysis of the problem to guide one to the relevant facts necessary to understand it clearly, i.e. "the problematic situation must be reduced to the relevant factual situation."[15] This may appear at first to be presumptive reasoning in which the very purpose of field work is being usurped. Far from it. It is rather an attempt to find out what facts are likely to be relevant to the solution of the problem and to determine from this what methods will be most effective in obtaining those facts. To enter the field without analysis of the problem may result in the arbitrary collection of data (some of which is likely

14. Northrop considers the first stage of inquiry to be both problem statement and analysis, through devoting two separate chapters to the matter.

15. Northrop, p. 34.

to be irrelevant) utilizing methods which may not be adequate for the problem at hand.

A careful analysis of the problem will assist the field worker in making the following determinations:

1. *Where fieldwork should be done*: Obviously one must select an area or areas which will fit the problem. A collector wishing to study the effect of commerical entertainment media on traditional forms of entertainment will not select a community which has not yet been electrified or where there are no radios, television sets, or phonographs.

2. *The probable time necessary for effective field work*: (To be dealt with in the next chapter).

3. *The materials and data relevant to the solution of the problem*: The materials and data which may be collected in any field situation are nearly infinite. The analysis of the problem should provide the criteria for selecting the relatively few items which are likely to be relevant to the problem. A collector wishing to make a study of the social contexts of story-telling is hardly likely to concern himself with children's riddling or singing games.

4. *The field methods most likely to be utilized in obtaining the relevant materials and data*: Different problems raise different methods, and there will be as many different methods (or combinations of methods) as there are fundamentally different kinds of problems.[16] If the problem analysis, for example, suggests certain technical field methods which the collector is incapable of handling, then he must obtain adequate training in the method, make arrangements

---

16. Northrop, p. 19, and Melville, G. Herskovits, "Some Problems of Method in Ethnography" in *Method and Perspective in Anthropology*, ed. Robert Spencer (Minneapolis, 1954), p. 6.

for the services of a person properly trained in that method, or alter his problem to one calling only for those methods which he can handle.

Problem statement and analysis alone will not guarantee the success of the field trip, for the problem of field work is essentially human, involving the ability of the field worker to adjust to new situations and to new personalities that express themselves in ways that may be different from those with which he is familiar.[17] When one adds the possibility of unforeseen events cropping up to affect the field situation, the problems of a field worker are such that only other field workers can fully appreciate them. The collector must be adaptable to the situation. He may have to use methods which he had not previously considered during the period of problem analysis, or he may have to improvise new methods as the situation demands. In some cases he may even have to alter his problem or replace it entirely. In consideration of this possibility, the field worker should have one or more alternate problems. But careful problem statement and analysis, supported by rigorous training in theory and method, should minimize the possibility of uncorrectable or insoluble error arising in the field.

4. The Kinds of Folklore Data

In stating the problem and in its analysis, the field worker may be assisted by a knowledge of the kinds of folklore "facts" or data which it is possible to collect, and the various kinds of problems (not the specific problems themselves) to which field work lends itself.

Folklore field data may be categorized as follows:

1. *Folklore materials*: Basic instruction in most undergraduate folklore courses should supply a collector

17. Herskovits, "Some Problems," p. 11.

with a good idea of the various kinds (genres and sub-genres) of folklore materials. An excellent conspectus of these may be found in Ó Súilleabháin's *Handbook*.[18]

2. *Folklore processes*: In addition to the actual manner in which folklore is transmitted, under this heading may be included the tradition bearers and the social and physical context involved in such transmission as well as the specific oral performance styles of folklore informants.

3. *Folklore ideas*: This category concerns the ideational concepts of tradition bearers about folklore, and includes their attitudes, feelings, themes, and aesthetics, as well as individual and group psychological and social reactions to the materials and situations of folklore.

In this work I will use the term *folklore data* or simply *data*, when referring to any of the kinds of folklore "facts" described above.

5. The Kinds of Folklore Field Problems

Despite the great number of folklore problems that could be posed for possible solution by field work, all will fall into one or another of three kinds of field collections:

1. Folklore data as they exist at present.

2. Folklore data involving the comparison of such data with similar data from the past (essentialy restudies of previously collected areas).

3. Folklore data as they exist at present for the purpose of historical reconstruction of the past (obtained through content analysis of the collected data).

18. Seán Ó Súilleabháin, *A Handbook of Irish Folklore* (Dublin, 1942, reprinted Hatboro, Pa., 1963).

This temporal scheme of field collections may be sub-divided further as to whether each of them is carried out in terms of (1) a single area, culture, group, or individual, or (2) a synchronic comparison involving two or more areas, cultures, groups, or individuals.

6. The Types of Collecting Projects

Thus far no descriptive terminology has been suggested for the various types of collecting projects. Such a typology, however, may ease the task of problem analysis in deter-mining the area to be studied and the time needed for effective field work. I believe the three types of collecting projects listed below cover every possible type:

1. *Survey projects*: As its name suggests, a sampling of the folklore repertory of one or more areas, cultures, groups, or individuals. Most collecting projects of the past have been of this order. Such surveys are needed for areas in which little or no previous collect-ing has been done. It is also a necessary preliminary step in the solution of more complex problems calling for field work.[19] Frequently these projects are carried out by genre specialists and will treat of only one genre, such as songlore, tales, or children's lore. Be-cause survey projects can usually be carried out quickly (depending, however, upon the vitality of tradition, the size of the population or the area to be covered, and the degree of comprehensiveness in-tended by the collector), such projects are usually undertaken by those who are able to collect only dur-ing their vacations from work. Survey projects are

19. For example, in my field work in the Buchan District of north-eastern Scotland in 1959-60, I first made a cursory survey of the folklore in central Buchan in order to have a comparative base for my study of one community in the area. This survey helped me to understand the idiosyncrasies of the specific community selected for study.

sometimes sarcastically referred to as "shotgun collecting" (describing the situation in which a collector attempts to collect as much folklore from as many people in as many places as it is possible to do in the least amount of time.)

2. *Depth projects*: The intensive collecting of all kinds of folklore data from one or more communities, groups, or individuals.[20] This type of project usually involves great expenditures of time and effort, and is feasible only where and when it is applied to small numbers of individuals. Depth collecting in populous communities is properly carried out by several individuals working as a team with each collector responsible for collecting only certain data from all the members of the community, or for collecting all the data from a small workable group of the population.

3. *Local projects*: Collecting one or more kinds of folklore data from one's own family, from neighbors, from children, or from local representatives of various trade, occupational, professional, or student groups. This type of project is ideal for training folklore students in field methods and in handling folklore data. It is also excellent therapy and practice for the folklorist who loves field work, but who is not able to go on extended field trips.

There is another type of collecting which, because it is unplanned, cannot properly be called a project type:

4. *Incidental collecting*: Collecting as the opportunity arises. Such collecting is unplanned and is the result

20. Herbert Halpert, "Folklore: Breadth versus Depth," *JAF* 71 (1958), pp. 97-103, makes a helpful distinction between depth collecting and breadth collecting, the latter consisting of collecting all kinds of folklore materials.

of a fortunate combination of unforeseen occurrences and the accidental presence of unusual tradition bearers.[21] On occasion such collecting may lead to the formulation of formal problems followed by organized field projects.

21. An example of this occurred in my own work in 1962 when an Indiana-born truck driver from Texas visited my home. In less than ten minutes of talking with him, I realized that he was an extremely talented story-teller. Out came the tape recorder, and in the few hours that he was in my home I collected some twelve superbly told tales, Texas boasts, truck driver's legends and superstitions, toasts, and a miscellany of other folklore materials.

CHAPTER III

Time
Considerations

ASIDE FROM A GENERAL AGREEMENT that longer field trips are better than short ones, the amount of time to be spent on a field project has been given too little attention by folklore field workers. At the same time it has been the subject of considerable controversy among anthropologists.[1] The reason for this difference in interest or concern between the two disciplines lies in their respective attitudes toward the priority of factors essential to problem solving. Anthropologists are usually able to state their problems and analyze them with a view to determining the time necessary to complete the project. Then they make financial and leave-time arrangements to fit the problem. Folklorists, less secure in their ability to obtain the necessary leave time and finances, frequently apply for both before problem analysis has been completed and then revise their problems to fit the time and finances which they have been able to obtain.

1. Melville J. Herskovits, "Some Problems of Method in Ethnography" in *Method and Perspective in Anthropology*, ed. Robert F. Spencer (Minneapolis, 1954), p. 7.

Because of this lack of control over essential pre-field factors, the folklorist is often forced to abandon the normal order of considerations in the scientific initiation of inquiry. However, increasingly during the past decade funds have become available from a wide variety of sources,[2] and university officials and department heads have been more responsive to requests for leave-time and funds for field work. As folklore achieves respect as a scholarly discipline, the problems of leave-time and finances will decrease in direct proportion. The matter of the time to be spent in the field will then be analyzed by folklorists in terms of the actual problem needs.

This chapter will indicate the various factors bearing upon the time aspect. These factors may be divided into:

1. Factors determined by the problem itself.

2. Factors involving the collector's personality, abilities, and experience.

3. Factors involving the actual field situation.

1. Factors Determined by the Problem Itself

The type of collecting project suggested by the problem analysis must be a major element in determining the time necessary for securing the desired data. Generally speaking, survey projects will require less time than depth projects. And, too, the degree of comprehensiveness intended by the field worker for either type of project may radically affect time considerations. Should the collecting project concern only one kind of folklore data, or only one genre of folklore, the time spent in the field should be less than

2. For example, from institutions, from private foundations (e.g. Ford, Rockefeller, and Guggenheim), from the government (Fulbright grants) and from graduate university department grants-in-aid.

that needed to make a study calling for the collecting of all kinds of folklore data or covering many folklore genres.

If the problem calls for a calendar type of study, requiring the collection of data on the annual round of customs,[3] the collector should be in the field for the full cycle of the year's activities. Though many data of this type can be collected by interviewing techniques requiring less than a full year's attendance in the field, the observation of such activities supported by interview data will probably result in a more complete and accurate picture.

A collector making a functional study of folklore should consider a year's field work as a minimum, since a good part of the time will have to be spent in collecting general ethnographic data, in addition to folklore. If, however, the area has previously been reported by an ethnographer, the folklore collector will need to collect considerably fewer data and can spend more time with folklore data themselves.[4]

Many depth projects, such as those involving the intensive study of the folklore of a small community, a family, or an individual, will first require making a survey of the larger surrounding area to be utilized as a comparative base for determining the representativeness of the folklore data collected from the object of the study.[5] Such a survey may take several months. If, however, collecting has previously been carried out in the area, then the survey

3. The British are especially fond of this type of study. See, for example, the *British Calendar Customs* series issued by The Folk-Lore Society, for *England,* ed. A. R. Wright and T. E. Lones, 3 vols. (London, 1936, 1938, 1940); for *Scotland,* ed. Mrs. M. Macleod Banks, 3 vols. (London, 1937, 1939, 1941); for *Orkney and Shetland,* ed. Mrs. M. Macleod Banks (London, 1940), and for the *Isle of Man,* ed. Cyril I. Paton (London, 1939). For a more recent series, see F. Marian McNeill, *The Silver Bough,* volumes two and three of which are *A Calendar of Scottish National Festivals* (Glasgow, 1959, 1961). All of these, however, constitute a secondary source of materials, as none of them involved collecting in the field by their authors and editors.

4. Herskovits, "Some Problems," pp. 8-9.

5. See Chapter II, note 19.

period may be reduced or eliminated entirely, depending upon how adequate a job was previously done and how many years have passed since the original survey was made.

2. Factors Involving the Collector's Personality, Abilities, and Experience

The collecting situation involves social interplay between human beings who begin as strangers and who must achieve some level of rapport sufficient for the collector to be able to observe what is going on and to ask (and get answers to) questions. Rapport achievement must be mutually motivated, but while it is not essential for the potential informant (who can continue to function in his own community without becoming friendly with the stranger), the collector must achieve rapport if he is to function in the community at a level which will permit him to collect data. How well he establishes rapport is dependent to no small degree upon his personality. And how quickly he establishes rapport will determine how much time he can spend on obtaining the data he seeks. A collector who is generally slow in establishing positive relationships must take that factor into account when determining the time to be spent in the field.

After rapport has been established, the speed with which the collector can obtain accurate data becomes an essential factor in the time he must spend in the field. The perceptiveness, flexibility, and insight of the collector are crucial.

> Alertness to cues . . . will in the case of one student permit work to be done in a shorter period than that of another who responds more slowly, but for whom a longer period of residence will permit the achievement of results of comparable worth.[6]

6. Herskovits, "Some Problems," p. 8.

The psychological make-up of the collector is equally crucial. A long stay in one place, working continually on one project, may create sufficient fatigue, tenseness, and insecurity in a collector to affect critically the nature and quality of his data.[7] And, too, there is always the danger that too long a stay with a friendly people will result in a secondary ethnocentrism setting in, in which the collector, through over-identifying with his informants, is no longer able to observe objectively or report the full content of his interviews.[8] The collector's knowledge of his ability to prevent this must be a guide to the longest time at which he can function properly in the field as a scientific field worker. For him the project should end at that point.

The collectors' ability to understand fully the language spoken around him should also be raised at this point. In Chapter One it was stated that a field worker in folklore was expected to know the language of the people from whom he was to do collecting. However, command of a language does not guarantee cultural comprehension. The collector must contend with the local dialect of a tongue which he knows in another form. In the poetic and prose renderings of his informants, as well as in conversation with them, he will come upon the turn of a phrase, of an idiom, of imagery, of nuance in thought patterns, which he must recognize and decipher. Language familiarity of this order takes time to achieve. The collector whose mind and ear are attuned to this level of language may rapidly pass the stage where he has to concentrate on dialect problems. The collector less talented in this direction will have to allow himself sufficient time to achieve such proficiency—time which will have to be added to the period necessary for him to collect his data.

7. Herskovits, "Some Problems," p. 8.
8. Herskovits, "Some Problems," p. 7.

Another important time factor involves the experience of the collector. If the collector has had considerable field experience, his knowledge of methods and techniques of collecting should enable him to save much time which would otherwise be spent in gingerly feeling his way around and learning by trial and error. This will especially be true if his previous collecting experience has been either in neighboring communities or in similiar communities removed from his present field site. And in the case of an inexperienced collector, the time in the field necessary for completion of a collecting project will be in inverse proportion to the rigorousness of his training in field methods and theory, other factors excluded.

3. Factors Involving the Actual Field Situation

The first two groups of factors involving the time considered necessary for proper field work centered on the problem set by the collector and on his personality, abilities, and experience. There is a third group of factors, totally removed from the collector himself, which has to do with the actual situation the collector finds, or expects to find, in the field.

Where the oral traditions of a community are vital, the collector may obtain sufficient data to answer his problem in a relatively short time. Where, however, the traditions are in flux and vast changes are being wrought in the internal scene by the introduction of outsiders, new ideas, technical know how, or mass communication media, it may take time to sift through the various layers of tradition.

The size of the population to be interviewed or the area to be covered may require travel and relocation time. If, however, there is sufficient homogeneity over a wide area or for large numbers of people, a sampling may be adequate for solving the problem.

In addition, the collector must take into account the specific group under study: "it is their preconceptions, their prejudices, their fears that dominate the scene."[9] His ability to work effectively in a community will depend upon the willingness of its members to allow him to do so. Nor will the collector's personality, experience, or training greatly affect a situation in which the inhabitants refuse to talk about, or allow him to observe, a specific ritual involving great secrecy. He may be able to get answers by indirection or deception, but this takes care and time—time which must be taken into consideration at the problem analysis stage (if the information of such secrecy is available at that point). On the other hand, in the case of a friendly people among whom much collecting has previously been done, the folk may be so familiar with collecting methods and so pleased to assist the field worker that they will ease the way for him and enable him to shorten his trip by many months.[10]

4. Miscellaneous Time Considerations

The collector is sometimes faced with a choice between a continuous period of residence in the field and shorter periods spread over a number of years. Here he must take into account the distance to be travelled to his field site (and the time necessary to do so), the need for re-establishment of rapport each time he arrives in the community, the attitudes of the inhabitants toward the occasional visitor, and the continuous time necessary to obtain certain data. These factors must, in turn, be balanced against the facts that studies of change over time

9. Melville J. Herskovits, *Man and His Works* (New York, 1950), p. 85.

10. Jean Ritchie, in personal conversation with me, described situations in her collecting in Ireland where the inhabitants of a house (who had previously been collected from by others) indicated to her exactly which corner of the room had the best acoustics for recording. This type of cooperation also reduced the time necessary to establish rapport.

are best carried out by several visits and that time away from the scene is needed for evaluation and digestion of materials already collected, or to allow for a period of rest and cooling off[11] both for the collector and his informants, especially where the work involves obtaining data available only through traumatic or dramatic disclosures and self-analysis, as well as to prevent secondary ethnocentrism from setting in.

Also to be considered in determining the time to be spent in the field are such unpredictable occurrences as the breakdown of equipment (perhaps requiring repair at some distance from the collecting site) and illness to the collector, members of his family, or some of his key informants.

Unless a collector is able to repair his own equipment, he should anticipate the loss of some time in the contingency of breakdown. And even should the collector be able to repair his own equipment, he may be delayed in doing so while he awaits the arrival of replacement parts from a distant factory or supplier. (For further comments on this problem, see the section on supplies and equipment in the next chapter).

Moving to a new environment frequently presents health hazards to the collector and his family. Temperature and humidity conditions present in the new surroundings may sap the strength and vitality with which the collector expected to attack his field problems. Impure water supplies or insects may cause sickness which, however temporary, will result in the loss of time in the field. Sudden attacks of ailments which are chronic to the collector may incapicitate him at crucial points in his

11. Ralph Piddington, *An Introduction to Social Anthropology*, Vol. II (Edinburgh, 1957), p. 539 states:

> . . . rest pauses during field-work are essential. The ethnographer should from time to time stand back from his material and cease his actual investigations for a period. Even to read novels or go shooting is helpful in this regard."

work. In the latter case, even perfect health at the time the trip is undertaken and periodic visits to local doctors will not prevent such attacks from occurring and the collector should allow for them in his time schedules. And should the collector have his family with him, it may be necessary for him to take off time from his collecting chores in order to minister to their possible illnessess. Nor can the collector be sure that key informants will stay healthy during his time in the field. He may be forced to bide his time until an informant gets well before continuing his work on a specific project. Though time losses can not be predicted for such occurrences, they must nevertheless be considered in the overall plans of the collector.

* * *

Awareness of all the above factors contributing to the time problem in field work will not in itself shorten the time necessary to do proper field work. Too many of these factors are almost wholly beyond the control of the collector, but by carefully weighing all these factors he should be able to make a more accurate estimation of the time he will need for his work.

CHAPTER IV

Pre-Field
Preparations

ONCE THE COLLECTOR IS IN THE FIELD he will be an extremely busy man. It will then be too late for him to catch up with many of the details and matters which he should have dealt with earlier. By tending to these before he enters the field situation, the collector will help to ease his entry into the field, insure himself of the maximum and most effective use of his limited time there, and help to prepare himself for certain eventualities which may prove handicapping or unpleasant should they crop up to catch the collector unaware in the field.

Pre-field preparations can usually be handled during the months available to the collector between the time he has committed himself to going into the field and his actual departure for it. Rarely are field trip decisions made on such short notice that the collector is forced to skip these preparations. In such cases even an experienced field worker will find himself considerably handicapped unless he has paid attention to at least an essential minimum of these details.

This chapter lists and describes the many details to which the collector should attend in pre-field preparations. Indeed, it may serve as a check-list for such preparations.

1. Available Literature

When possible, the collector should acquaint himself fully with the literature on the area and its people.[1] Such published materials will supply him with information on the social history, occupational habits, education, religion, economy, and politics of his informants-to-be. Equally important will be those details concerning the area to be visited, including geography, weather conditions, available food sources and supplies, location of towns and cities, and road conditions. All this information will help him to prepare for social contacts, a division of his time in the field, and the kinds of supplies and travel plans essential to speed his work along.

No less important is information of the specific folklore which is known to exist or has been collected in the area. Where the area has been surveyed previously by professional folklorists or anthropologists, such data could save him much time in the field and help him to avoid duplicating the efforts of others.[2] It may also suggest special problems to be dealt with, and later serve as a check on his own investigations. If the data are scanty or the work of non-professionals, the collector may still be able to obtain some idea of what work is needed to solve his problems, as well as an idea of the kinds of materials in the area for which he can prepare to look when in the field.

1. *Notes and Queries on Anthropology*, 6th edition (London, 1951), p. 28; also Maud Karpeles, ed., *The Collecting of Folk Music and Other Ethnomusicological Material: A Manual for Field Workers* (London, 1958), p. 8.
2. Karpeles, p. 8.

In searching for literature on the area or culture to be visited, the collector will, in a sense, be preparing a working bibliography. In assembling his bibliography he should make certain he has covered the lesser sources as well as those more obvious ones which will come to hand almost immediately. The list below is given as an aid in suggesting sources:

1. Published folklore collectanea and data, including books and journals, not only in the field of folklore itself, but in related fields such as literature, anthropology, history, languages, linguistics, and sociology,
2. General cultural studies.
3. Local antiquarian publications.
4. Miscellanea of local societies.
5. Travel guides.
6. Travel journals and reminiscences.
7. Governmental publications (e.g. health, census, and economic reports).
8. Histories—national and local.
9. Popular magazines.
10. Newspapers—especially those local to the area.
11. Published diaries, biographies, and reminiscences of local inhabitants.
12. Novels by local authors based on local life.
13. Dictionaries, especially dialect dictionaries.

The collector will not be able to obtain many of these works at the libraries to which he has access, but they should be listed for future reference. Often he will not even be aware of the existence of these materials until he gets into the field. This should not deter him in the preparation of his bibliography. Indeed, such a work is in itself an extremely valuable project and one for which his fellow folklorists will thank him.

Not only should the collector familiarize himself with as much of this literature as possible, but he should also make a selection from among these which he believes to be the major sources of useful information and secure copies of these to take into the field. Such works, especially those containing collectanea, will frequently serve the collector as sources for questions to be asked or from which finding lists and questionnaires can be prepared.

2. Contacting Collectors

Field workers are strongly advised to get in touch with any collector who has worked in the area planned for a field trip. In most cases such a person will turn out to be the best possible source of information about the place and its inhabitants, especially if his field work was done in fairly recent years. Also, considerable information which never gets published is in his keeping, and may help the stranger to avoid making *faux pas* in the new society which he is entering, as well as informing him which collecting methods work best, which subjects are taboo, and which social classes are to be avoided on initial contacts, among other suggestions. Most important of all, he can usually supply names and addresses of potential informants or official contacts, and may be persuaded to write to these people and assist in easing a collector's way into the community.[3]

The International Folk Music Council manual advises collectors that "courtesy and economy of effort suggest that [one] should normally avoid working in the field in which another collector is still active."[4] Occasionally, however, a specific problem calls for work in an area in which there is

3. In my collecting experiences in Scotland, the generous help of Hamish Henderson proved invaluable in preparing me for my field work in Aberdeenshire.
4. Karpeles, p. 8.

another collector. In such a case, the incoming collector should contact the resident collector to obtain his approval and to make friends. There is more than courtesy involved here. If the resident collector has set up good relations with the inhabitants of the area, he can, if he has a mind to do so, make it literally impossible for the incoming collector to work effectively there. A friend in the field, on the other hand, can smooth the way, make field work easier and pleasanter, and considerably shorten the period of rapport establishment. And there is always the good possibility that the coordinated activities of two collectors in the same area will so perfectly complement and supplement each other that the total achievement of the two will add up to more than simply the sum of their individual efforts.

3. Contacts with Leading Personalities in the Region

While it is not always possible to do so before entering the field, the collector should attempt to reach local people who may assist him with his project. Though local government officials, ministers, doctors, teachers, librarians, and the like, will usually be unable to supply the collector with the materials for which he is searching (indeed, they may not even be aware of them), they may serve in establishing good will with local people.[5] In any case they can often supply the collector with details of existing local conditions which will help in his coming settlement in the area.

5. Caution should be used, however. Benjamin D. Paul, "Interview Techniques and Field Relationships" in *Anthropology Today* (Chicago, 1953), p. 430 comments:

> Whether he [the field worker] asks them [local officials, etc.] to provide an introduction will depend on his estimation of how such auspices will promote or prejudice his standing in the community to be studied.

4. Existing Records and Films Made in the Region

If collecting has recently been done in the area, the incoming collector should make an effort to see and hear any films or tape recordings made there. If proper relations have been set up with previous collectors, or if the materials are located at some national or regional archives, this can usually be arranged, and the collector would be wise to spend as much time as possible in digesting such materials. Through them he should be able to get a first-hand idea of the kinds of tradition which exist, the vitality of such traditions, and information which will help him to assess the linguistic situation. The latter may save him some time in mastering the peculiarities of the local dialect, as well as help him to ascertain the difference between normal speech and performance patterns.[6]

5. Supplies and Equipment

An important part of the records made in the field will be in the form of notes. The collector should be sure to prepare an adequate supply of notebooks and pads to carry him through his stay in the region. For most immediate notetaking in the field, the best notepaper would be that which is capable of taking either ink or pencil, and is of a size which can fit into one's pocket. Generally speaking, pads of three-by-five note paper will be adequate for most purposes. In addition the collector should prepare sufficient supplies of large (8½ by 11), lined pads to be used in copying field notes, as well as for transcribing texts from

6. For example, prior to my field work in Aberdeenshire I spent as much time as was available at the School of Scottish Studies listening to tapes of field recordings from the area in which I was to do my collecting. This experience helped me in understanding the various forms which the local dialect took in normal speech and performance.

recordings. If the field worker takes notes and records texts in shorthand, he should be sure to have a supply of shorthand pads available.

Hardcovered notebooks to be used for diary notes should also be stocked, as well as datebooks for appointments. In cases where experienced collectors have worked up various forms for different kinds of data, these should be printed or mimeographed and a sufficient supply prepared for the duration of the field trip.

Proper equipment for recording and filming informants and data should be selected and readied for the trip sufficiently in advance of departure for the field to assure adequate time for testing and practicing with the equipment. The actual selection of such equipment should be given thought and attention. Advice on equipment can be obtained from other collectors, from various trade guides and magazines, from technical articles specifically intended for collectors and written by experienced field workers,[7] and from catalogues and specification sheets supplied by manufacturers of tape recorders and photographic equipment. The first consideration in the selection of equipment must be quality, durability, and weight, with cost an important, but secondary, consideration.

The collector should obtain certain technical information regarding the area in which he will be recording. If the area is only partly electrified, it may be necessary for him to have two recording machines, one a self-powered battery recorder and the second a recorder which can work off a main power supply. For the latter it will be necessary to know the type of current (AC or DC), the voltage and the frequency available, and the equipment will have to be supplied with necessary converters and transformers. In

7. See, for example, Alan P. Merriam, "The Selection of Recording Equipment for Field Use," *Kroeber Anthropological Society Papers*, No. 10 (Berkeley, 1954), pp. 5-9; also Karpeles, pp. 9-13.

areas where voltage changes occur during different hours of the day, the transformer should have rheostat controls to allow for the fluctuating power.[8] A tuning fork, pitch pipe, or some instrument with a known absolute pitch should be included in the supplies; it will come in handy for setting a control pitch so that should the recordings be made under conditions which will vary the speed of the tape, on playing it back away from the field the speed of the tape can be adjusted to the standard to guarantee an exact reproduction of the sounds actually recorded in the field. Information on weather conditions will be important in the selection of recording tape as well as for its storage. Tape manufacturers will gladly supply specifications and information on which tapes are most suitable for various climates and weather conditions.

The collector should also learn the availability of spare parts and repair facilities. In any case, he should familiarize himself with the mechanical workings of his equipment sufficient to allow him to make at least minor repairs. Time can be lost in the field when equipment has to be sent away for repairs.

When possible, the collector should have two machines in the field. One can act as a safety to be used if the other machine breaks down. It can also be used for making safety copies of the collector's recordings, or to be lent to informants in certain situations in which they prefer not to record materials or information in the collector's presence.

The collector should practice as often as possible with his equipment to be sure he knows how to get recordings of optimum quality. Machines are no better than the technicians who run them, and once in the field it is too late to achieve such proficiency. Too many field workers

8. In the Buchan District of Aberdeenshire, for example, power varies from 180 to 230 volts according to the time of day and the draw on the central power station.

treat their equipment as troublesome adjuncts to field work, and care little for the quality of their recordings as long as they are audible and transcriptions can be made from them. Yet these same collectors work extremely hard to insure the fidelity and exactness of their handwritten notes. Essentially there is no difference between the two forms of data taking. Both should be treated with equal care. Indeed, the very fact that the recording machine adds a dimension (that of sound) to the collected data should be reason enough for even more painstaking care in the making of full quality recordings.

The same care should be applied to the selection and use of photographic equipment. Still and motion pictures (with or without sound) of informants, places, and things are an important part of field data. In many cases they represent the only way in which the actuality of the field situation can be communciated to others.[9]

Collectors should remember that every recording and photograph is a piece of objective data that can be re-examined without change at many levels for many different types of analyses, not only by the collector himself but by others as well. These materials, in the form of recordings and photographs, are the fundamental data for the emerging science of folklore. Though they may be subject to various and changing interpretations in the course of analysis, the recordings and photographs remain constant as objective reports of existing facts at the time of collection.

6. The Collector's Repertory of Folklore

If he does not already have a repertory of stories, songs, and riddles, the collector should learn some. They may come in very handy in socializing with informants. The

9. For an excellent discussion of the use of films in collecting, see David Rycroft's instructions in Karpeles, pp. 32-40.

collector will perhaps find that his informants are tired of having the entertainment move in only one direction and may call on him to entertain them. Such a repertory may also aid in drawing out materials from those reticent to perform before a stranger.[10] And in the collecting of certain materials (such as obscene folklore), the field worker will frequently be able to break down his informant's reserve by first performing such materials himself.

Though certain schools frown on the performing of guitar- and banjo-playing folklorists, experience shows that these people sometimes turn out to be excellent collectors because of their ability to communicate effectively with informants in terms of knowledge of actual performance. In the collecting situation, however, such performances must be kept within the bounds dictated by the informants and by the good manners and sense of the collector himself.[11]

* * *

While any of the above preparations for field work will help the collector in carrying out his mission, certain ones should certainly have priority over others, especially in those rare cases where field trip decisions are made on such short notice that the collector cannot tend to all of them. In such cases the collector is advised to attend first to the preparations relating to supplies and equipment, and, if

10. See Richard Bauman, "Y. L. Cahan's Instructions on the Collecting of Folklore," *NYFQ* 18 (1962), p. 286.

11. I refer here, of course, to professionally trained folklorists. Samuel B. Charters, "Some Do's and Don't's of Field Recording," Vol. 12, No. 3, of *Sing Out*, p. 53, described the dangers of performance by untrained field workers: "If you're a poor performer the folk artist loses some of the respect he might have had for you, and if you're a good performer then he becomes self conscious . . . the nervous old guitar player from the small mountain town who hasn't been playing lately and never did play very well will just be upset by the collector who wants to show off how well he can play. If you insist on playing for people then you're not really interested in collecting."

possible, to then contact folklore collectors who have preceded him or are still resident in the area he has chosen for his field work. Any of the other preparations may be waived, but with the full knowledge that to do so will handicap the collector and probably add several months to the time he will need in the field to complete his project.

CHAPTER V

Rapport Establishment
and Maintenance[1]

ONCE THE COLLECTOR REACHES THE REGION in which his
field work is to be done, he must be guided by one objective: to establish rapport as quickly as possible and to
maintain such rapport throughout the duration of his stay.
Without rapport his project can not be carried out; with
it he is at least sure that he will be able to work as
effectively as his training and his time in the field will
permit. There is, however, no method for establishing
rapport. No two situations in the field are identical; no
collector is like any other collector; no informant or group
of informants reacts to the collecting situation as does any
other. These truisms form the essence of the problem of

1. For the general outline and some of the best ideas in this chapter
I am grateful to the paper by Benjamin D. Paul on "Interview Techniques and Field Relationships" in *Anthropology Today*, ed. A. L.
Kroeber (Chicago, 1953), pp. 430-451. My own field work, experiments
in finding adequate methods for folklore collecting was strongly influenced by this article soon after its publication date. In borrowing the
techniques and ideas suggested therein, I attempted to apply them
wholly to the task of satisfying the needs of the folklorist and his problems, rather than simply having the folklorist become an ethnologist when
in the field.

47

rapport establishment. The personal factor rules the scene. The intelligent, personable, sociable, and sensitive person will find his own way to establish the relationships necessary for him to achieve his goal. The exact manner in which he does so will be guided by his problem, by the time he has to spend in the field, by his knowledge of his own personality, and by his ability to recognize cues to the personality of his potential informants. Though there are no methods for establishing rapport, there are extrapersonal factors which can be dealt with in discussing the problem.

1. Locating Living Quarters

The first of the collector's activities in the community necessarily involves his finding a place to settle. In depth projects, or those involving areas of rather small compass, the collector must pay careful attention to this matter, for the place he selects should serve as his headquarters for the full duration of his stay.

His headquarters should be centrally located (permitting easy access to all parts of the community) and situated so that the collector's activities will be as conspicuous as possible. A large part of rapport establishment involves the collector's being seen frequently enough by the inhabitants for them to become used to his presence and to begin to accept him as a natural part of the local scene.

The community selected for settlement should be typical of the entire region in which collecting is to take place. If the collector is unable to travel to his informants because of inclement weather, he should be able to work effectively in his own community and avoid wasting time while waiting for weather conditions to improve. If the collector's project involves work in a rural country area, he should attempt to locate in a small town nearby in which he will be able to obtain living supplies and be within easy reach of the outlying areas. Location at a place out in the country will make him less accessible to his informants. And, ideally, he should be situated on or near a relatively good travelling road, should his work take him outside the immediate area.

In selecting a place to settle, the collector may obtain assistance from some of the inhabitants of the community. If pre-field preparations were completed and the collector has been in touch with local citizens, such persons can be helpful in house-hunting. And it will also aid in rapport establishment if the collector makes it plain by seeking such aid that he is dependent upon the local citizenry. If they have a part in his very first steps in the community, they are likely to feel responsible for him from that point on.

In the actual house selection, however, the collector cannot relinquish the final decision to those whom he has called on to assist him. He must use his own good sense and experience in making sure that they do not place him so that he is cut off from any part of the citizenry which may be important to his project.

The first tendency of local persons in authority would be to place the stranger in as grand a house as possible. This, however, might give him a status which could reflect negatively in his reaching people at the low end of the social-economic ladder. Nor, in most circumstances, should he make the mistake of moving to the wrong side of the tracks, thereby perhaps alienating the official level of society; instead he should attempt to settle in a house which represents the average mode of existence for the community. Circumstances will vary, of course, from situation to situation so that these suggestions may not apply for every field experience. For example, some particular problem possibly may be solved only by moving to the wrong side of the tracks. In other cases the collector may have to move into rather meagre quarters simply because no other housing is available.

The collector can direct house-hunting activity in such a way as to make it appear as if his local assistants have actually chosen his headquarters for him. When they direct him to a grand mansion, he may indicate that it is too large, too expensive, too drafty, or too distant to serve him adequately. Similarly, a mean house is too small, too drafty, or too far from the main activity. Eventually he will be led to a livable structure which will serve his purposes, and which is acceptable to those levels of the local citizenry which he is trying to reach. In a highly stratified society it may not always be apparent at first glance which mode of existence is average, and the collector should move slowly until he has had a chance to size up the situation. Usually there will be no problem in identifying the élite and the lower strata, but the various groups in between may not reveal themselves so readily. A trip through the community with casual friendliness will aid in solving the problem. Where the society is relatively homogeneous, there will be fewer gross differences among the citizenry and the collector can make his choice of housing with less concern.

Should the collector's project call for much travelling over long distances with only short stops in any one place (as in some survey projects), he cannot be expected to approach the problem of housing in the same manner. For the most part, he simply will not have the time to make a truly careful selection at any of his stops. He should, however, still locate his headquarters as centrally as possible in each community, allowing for the greatest conspicuousness. This may consist of any centrally located inn, private residence, hotel, or motel.

None of this advice will apply when a folklorist is able to do collecting only on weekends or days off from work.

He is then forced to travel out from an already established abode in a city or town not too distant from the communities in which he will be collecting.

2. Transportation

Though the collector is advised to make himself as conspicuous as possible, he must do so as unostentatiously as possible. If the average person in the community does most of his travelling by foot, by public transportation, or by using an older model car, the collector should stick as close to this norm as possible. To travel around in a new, mile-long Cadillac or fancy sports car will immediately type the collector as a show-off, a vacationer, or worse. An inexpensive old-model auto, plain luggage, and a minimum of supplies and equipment will help to type the collector as a reasonable kind of fellow. All too often the stereotype of the Outsider in the image of the vacationer is of such a negative order that the collector is first forced to erase such an image before he can proceed further with rapport establishment.

3. Role Playing

Whether by design or not, the collector is forced to assume a role in the community from the moment he makes first contact with it. The potential roles he may play are limited, first, to those which he is willing and able to play, and second, to the range of roles which the community is willing to allow him to play. His role must fit into those areas in which his intentions and ability overlap the community's expectations of him.[2] The assumption of any role outside this limited range is fraught with danger for the collector's project, and he must pre-

2. Paul, p. 431.

pare to change the project if his own role selection does not fit in with the wishes and understanding of the community.

The collector's statement to his potential informants that he is a folklorist will make little or no sense to most of his auditors.[3] Even in relatively sophisticated societies the term is too little known generally to have any meaning. The collector should instead stress some aspect of his work which will be familiar and understandable to the majority of the community. His mission can be stated without the use of any technical jargon: "I'm interested in writing a book of the beautiful old stories told here," or "I'm getting up an old-fashioned songbook in order that our children may be able to sing the old ballads."[4] The combination of a simple statement and flattery may smooth the way to initial acceptance.

In a community in which the citizens are aware of differences between their own traditions and those of others, the collector's statement that he wishes to study those differences may suffice.[5] Or he may indicate that he wishes to learn the local dialect, which immediately places his informants in the position of experts and readily leads to the collecting of song and tale texts. Once confidence is gained in this manner, the collector may broaden his project to include such data as customs and beliefs, which may be explained with the statement that the songs and

3. Dorothy Scarborough, *From a Southern Porch* (New York, 1919), pp. 57-58, cites her own error in using the word *folklore* and the lack of understanding of the term by several of her informants. Folklorists have frequently commented on the error of using the term when collecting; see, for example, Louis C. Jones, "A Student Guide to Collecting Folklore," *NYFQ* 2 (1946), p. 152.

4. Vance Randolph, *Ozark Folksongs* (Columbia, Missouri, 1946), Volume I, p. 32.

5. C. G. Seligmann in a note on collecting, in *Folk-Lore* 13 (1902), p. 311, recommends that the collector seeking information about games, arts, crafts etc., say something to this effect: "Different people do these things differently, and I want to see how your method differs from ours."

tales need to be placed in a context which will be meaningful to others.[6]

Before assuming certain roles, it is well to know what the attitudes of the community toward those roles are likely to be. When I was doing field work in parts of North Carolina, it could have been disastrous to my project had I indicated that I was connected with a school, university, or any educational institution. Their longtime suspicion of educators who wanted to improve conditions and an inferiority complex developed through the stereotyped "hillbilly" connotations which were usually attached to them by tourist agencies and commercial exploiters in their own area, left them totally cold to outside "smart-boys." Northeastern Scotland, on the other hand, offers no difficulties whatsoever over the educational affiliations of collectors. The Scots countryman admires education and learning, and affiliation with a Scottish university helped to open many doors for me.

Nationalism may also assist in the establishment of rapport. In some countries the field worker who stresses that he is collecting old traditions so that a record may be kept for all time usually need not go any further, especially if he can show his affiliation with a national cultural body. The intense cultural nationalism of small countries is especially conducive to such an approach.[7]

On the other hand, mention of affiliation with a national or federal body may prove an impassable obstacle in some places. Where the local citizens indulge in illegal or semilegal activities (as in the case of moonshining by southern mountaineers in the United States or poaching by gypsies and tinkers in Britain), any representative of the govern-

6. Paul, p. 432.

7. For comments on nationalism as a factor in collecting folklore, see Stith Thompson, ed., *Four Symposia on Folklore* (Bloomington, Indiana, 1953), pp. 89-90, 156, 169.

ment is mistakenly considered a law-enforcement officer. And in areas which are anti-government because of their refusal to follow certain national policies (as in many southern communities in the United States), federal connections will only erect a high wall between the collector and some of his potential informants.

The role of historian is usually a good one to adopt. The collector may stress that he is not interested in official history such as one finds in books, but rather is interested in local ideas about history which can be found in the stories and songs which the people tell or sing. Using this approach in eastern Massachusetts, I was able to obtain wonderful examples of traditional folk history, from which I was able to lead my informants into reciting other kinds of traditions. However, even the role of historian may be misunderstood, as in the case of a young anthropologist who used this tack in a South American community only to be deluged by local experts, genealogists, clippings, relics, etc., and thereby found his personal contacts considerably restricted.[8]

If the collector fails to make his role apparent to a community shortly after his arrival, the community may do it for him. Sometimes, the role assigned to him by the community, when it is not an onerous one, can be profitably used by the collector. Richard Dorson, for example, was assumed to be a "writer feller" (because of the elbow patches on the sleeves of his jacket) in a northern Negro community. The role was one which he successfully adopted in securing a large number of tale texts.[9] Frequently, however, the role assigned by the community is one which the collector cannot relish and to which the community strenuously objects. Should a community decide that the collector is a government officer, the effects

8. Referred to in Paul, pp. 432-433.
9. Richard M. Dorson, *Negro Folktales in Michigan* (Cambridge, Mass., 1956), p. 4.

can be disastrous to the work or to the collector.[10] And in small gossip-ridden communities, the motives of the collector may be incorrectly interpreted and he may be viewed as a loose man, a white slaver, or worse. The collector is usually better off if he sets the role which he wishes to assume.

Sometimes the assumption of a role needs supporting evidence to be convincing. An introduction to the community by a collector who has previously done work there can smooth the way and establish the collector's role immediately. Pre-field contact with some local figures may serve the same purpose. Or if the collector has been unable to make any pre-field contacts, he may look up one of the better educated members of the community after he gets there (such as the local doctor, priest, or a school teacher) and through discussion of the matter they may be able to decide what role it would be best for the collector to assume, after which the newly found contact can make arrangements for the collector to be introduced in that role.

The collector who arrives in a community with his wife and children will be less suspect to its citizens. He immediately identifies himself as a married man and a person of responsibility. A single man may be viewed as a not particularly safe addition to the community and, when it comes time for him to begin searching out informants, he may find that in order to get to female tradition bearers he first will have to work through the male members of a family. He will have to pass inspection while they ascertain that he has no designs on their womenfolk. A visit by a single male to a rural household in the middle of the day when only the farm wife or kitchen maid

10. Emelyn E. Gardner, *Folklore from the Schoharie Hills, New York* (Ann Arbor, Mich., 1937), p. 2, describes a situation in which she was charged with being a "guvment spy" and threatened with "the black bottle" containing "poison or something, which they refused to explain."

is at home may be met with a cold rebuff and an invitation to return when "the man" is at home. But the field worker who brings along a small child or who has his wife on his arm is likely to be welcomed in for a cup of coffee or tea, and the collector is able to begin his work almost immediately. And, of course, there are certain areas of superstition and custom of which it would be most difficult for any male to obtain knowledge, but which a woman, because of her sex, would have no difficulty whatsoever in obtaining; menstrual lore and child-bearing beliefs, among others, are best left to a collector's wife or female assistant to obtain, even if she has had little or no prior experience in the field.[11]

In assuming a role the field worker should attempt to do so in such generalized terms that he will be able to enlarge the scope of his work when and if he has to. By means of such generalization he should be able to change his role at a later date after some degree of rapport has been achieved. If the collector takes on any role other than folklorist or collector, he should leave the way open to reveal his actual role at a later date when he has achieved generalized acceptance[12] and his informants are better able to understand the import of his work. The change in role should be a gradual one which will leave no one with the feeling of having been deceived.

4. The Morality of Role Playing

The problem of role assumption must eventually lead one to question its morality. Where the field worker

11. My wife has always proved an excellent field worker in obtaining certain items of lore which I would not be able to get from female informants. The fact that she has many experiences in common with other women assists her in her inquiries. The empathic rapport between women comes, of course, from their sharing problems and roles. With experience, she has come to recognize many techniques and methods to be used in such contacts.

12. O. A. Oesar, "The Value of Team Work and Functional Penetration as Methods in Social Penetration," Chapter XVI in *The Study of Society: Methods and Problems* (London, 1939), p. 412.

admits openly that he is a folklorist (no matter what terms he uses to describe his role), there is no question of ethics involved, for he plays the role which is rightfully his. Where, however, an assumed role is taken on, the collector is involved in a deception. To be sure, it is a harmless deception intended solely for the purpose of allowing the collector to achieve maximum rapport. It is a question of personal values and each collector must answer it according to his own conscience. Most collectors will dismiss the matter after a little thought, and no longer be troubled by it.

The collector, however, should not assume that the commission of innocent deceptions of this order permits him to commit deceptions of a much more serious nature. In his dealing with people in the field he must occasionally unearth personal data which, if revealed, might harm his informants. Sometimes his informants may mistakenly believe that the identification of their names with certain materials or data will be harmful. Real or imagined, the collector owes it to his informants to protect them as they see fit. In such cases, the collector's choices are limited as to how he may present his information. He may omit the names of his informants, give them pseudonyms, or altogether avoid presenting his data. Some collectors simply rationalize the matter by assuming that their informants will never read the published reports.[13] This, perhaps, stems from the belief (conscious or unconscious) that their informants are illiterate, ignorant, or non-readers. Others collectors simply omit the names of all their informants.[14]

13. Richard M. Dorson, at the American Folklore Society meeting in Philadelphia, December 28, 1960, stated that since informants never read folklore journals or books there was no reason why sources could not be identified with the obscene materials collected from them.

14. For example, Melville J. and Frances S. Herskovits, *Dahomean Narrative: A Cross-Cultural Analysis* (Evanston, Ill., 1958), p. vi, write: "We should have liked to name here the individual narrators. Over the years, however, we have held to our pledge to those who have worked with us in the field not to identify them by name."

However, the collector must remember that his informants have egos not unlike his own, and that they may achieve great satisfaction in knowing that their names and contributions are recorded in print. The collector is then faced with the necessity of publishing only that information which is acceptable to his informants and suppressing or disguising any data which they believe may put them in a bad light. While scientific honesty and objectivity demand that he omit no pertinent data, moral courtesy demands that he not identify his informants with certain data. The collector must solve the dilemma by means which will satisfy both his scientific objectives and his humanistic ethics. Specific details with which his informants do not wish to be identified may be presented in a generalized context without identification of exact sources. In doing so, however, the collector must not impose his own standards on the materials and data but should use his informants' concepts of them. Too often slightly off-color materials have been omitted because the collector thought his informants would not want to be identified with them, when in fact they might not have minded it in the least. In other cases the collector has seen no reason for not specifically identifying certain materials with their sources only to find later that his informants were considerably angered by the action. But whichever solution the collector arrives at when presenting and interpreting his data, the course open to him in the field must be a basically honest one. He must not deceive his informants merely to obtain their materials, and then turn around after he has left the field to connect them with materials with which they would not care to be identified. Indeed, the problem here is not only one of honesty and ethics, but rather of a realistic consideration of the effects of such an action on future collecting projects. Not only will the collector make it impossible for himself to return to that area, but he may also make it impossible for any other collector to work there for many years to come.[15]

5. Establishing Initial Rapport

Establishment of rapport with individuals is so largely dependent upon the personalities involved that few general rules can be laid down. Experienced collectors have suggested that the pace of the initial meeting should be set by the informant, with the field worker bringing up the object of his visit ever so circuitously.[16] The psychology of collecting is much more complex than that, however. No two informants, even in the same region or family, will react identically and, indeed, on different occasions the same informant is likely to act in totally different ways.

In some cases an informant will engage the collector in a prolonged conversation about everything under the sun. This is usually his only immediate way of "sizing up" the collector. When the informant is satisfied with what he has heard, he may suddenly break off social conversation in mid-course and revert at once to the matters which concerned the collector. Such conversations may last for hours before the informant is satisfied, but the time spent may be richly rewarding to the patient collector.

15. This matter has been aired at some length in the articles of Herbert Halpert ("Folklore and Obscenity: Definitions and Problems," pp. 190-194) and Horace P. Beck ("Say Something Dirty!" pp. 195-199) in *JAF* 75 (1962), in a "Symposium on Obscenity in Folklore." The matter is perhaps best summarized by Halpert's statement:

In dealing with obscenity, as with any other lore regarded as sacred or secret, the collector has an obligation not to publish anything that would jeopardize the reputation or standing of an informant with his own people. Here . . . the collector must have in mind his responsibility to his colleagues in folklore, since tactless publication, like tactless behavior in the field, may make it impossible for another folklorist ever to collect in that area. (p. 193).

16. See, for example, Vance Randolph, *Ozark Folksongs*, Vol. I, pp. 31-32; W. Roy Mackenzie, *The Quest of the Ballad* (Princeton, 1919), pp. 20-21.

In other cases, just the collector's statement of his role will be sufficient to start an informant reciting tales and singing songs. In northeastern Scotland, one of my informants was ready and willing to sing for me from the moment I mentioned my project of collecting old songs and stories. He was so impatient to record his excellent repertory that he was unable to wait for the appointment I made with him. He came to my house later that day and began to sing the first group of more than 80 ballads which I was to obtain from him. Thereafter, he would drop into the house at any time of the day or night to record for me the songs he had recalled since our previous meeting.

Other singers and storytellers in the same region were more reluctant to part with their materials. My finest informant was willing to give me all that she could remember of her huge repertory of tales, rhymes, games, superstitions, and miscellaneous other lore, but refused to permit me to record her songs and ballads. Since I knew that she had such materials and was an excellent singer (she occasionally performed them in my presence when I left the tape recorder at home), I pursued the matter continuously. Two months after I made her acquaintance, she permitted me to record the first song. From then on the ballads and songs flowed forth at almost every session I spent with her. During the next eight months, I collected over 200 songs and ballads from this woman and even on my last day in Aberdeenshire she recorded several songs for me which I had not previously obtained from her.

Other collectors have had similar experiences. Vance Randolph, for example, states: "It is a peculiar fact that, the ice once being broken, a singer will usually run through his whole repertoire without much further urging; if you can get him to sing one song, the entire stock is yours for the asking."[17] This, however, should not be

17. Randolph, *Ozark Folksongs*, Vol. I, p. 32.

taken as a cue for the collector to press his fortune too hard. An unthinking collector, under the magic spell of the collecting session, may work his informants so hard that they become physically exhausted. Such actions may be rationalized in the case of older informants with a statement to the effect that one never knows when they might die and that it is best to get the materials while the getting is good. Rarely, however, does, a collector ever have an informant die "in his hands" while in the field. And I have met several informants who resisted later collectors because an earlier field worker had ruthlessly worked them for five or six hours running. In the excitement of performing their wares for the interested collector, an informant will indeed satisfy the driving needs of the folklorist. But in carrying out the task, the informant may become so exhausted that on later thinking about the situation he or she is sufficiently incensed as to assume that all collectors are equally inconsiderate. For this reason, as well as for the purpose of establishing the kind of rapport which will permit him to obtain those materials which reflect deeper feelings and hidden attitudes, the collector is advised to conduct his work almost leisurely, and to spread his time with any one informant over many short meetings.[18]

When collectors develop an interest in the major tradition bearer in a family, they sometimes unconsciously make the error of establishing rapport with that person alone and pay considerably less attention to other members of the family. The collector is well advised to establish full rapport with every member of the family, including spouses, children, and other relatives living in or near

18. This matter has not been sufficiently commented upon by collectors. However, B. A. Botkin, *Supplementary Instructions to The American Guide Manual: Manual for Folklore Studies* (n.p., 1938), p. 11, states: "Do not tire the informant. After an hour or so, it is often best to stop. Two or three visits are usually better than one."

their home. In regions in which religion has driven secular singing from the neighborhood, a member of a family may be induced to perform for a collector, only to be overruled by some other person in the family.[19] While this type of opposition cannot always be won over by the collector, he should make an attempt to do so simply by paying as much attention to other members of the household as is paid to the main informant therein. In northeastern Scotland I was directed to a family who were followers of an evangelistic sect that prohibited any kind of secular performance. Expecting the kind of negative reception which I had sometimes run across in collecting from similar sects in North Carolina, I was careful to pay even more attention to the informant's wife than I did to the informant himself. My plan, such as it was, worked admirably, and the man was permitted to perform his songs for me. On my third visit to the house, he confided to me: "Ye dee hae a wye wi' the wifie. She's aye fair scunnert fen I sing tae masel' or ma freends, but she disna mind a weet fen I sing tae yersel'."

Establishing good relations with all members of a family can pay still other dividends. When an elderly informant is found to be excellent, too little attention is usually paid to the younger members of the household. Frequently the collector's inquiry for other tradition bearers in a house stops when he is informed that "nobody else sings (or tells stories) here." Sometimes it is simply a case of a tradition in which no one will compete with an expert performer out of respect (or fear) of his reputation.[20]

19. See, for example, Emelyn E. Gardner & Geraldine J. Chickering, *Ballads and Songs of Southern Michigan* (Ann Arbor, Mich., 1939), pp. 10-11; Dorothy Scarborough, *A Song Catcher in Southern Mountains* (New York, 1937), pp. 29-30.

20. William Hugh Jansen, "From Field to Library" in *Folk-Lore* 63 (1952), p. 154, comments: " . . . the folk listen to a real artist; they would never think of competing with him, for it would be judged 'no contest'."

Younger members of the family may indeed have repertories of their own which they can perform well enough, but these traditions usually lie dormant or inactive as long as the older performer lives; only after his death will the younger performers come to the fore to assume his mantle.[21] By establishing good rapport with these younger tradition bearers it may be possible to get them to perform their repertories when the old man isn't around.

Many collecting projects involve short-term collecting spread out over large areas. Here the problem of rapport establishment is of a different order. The travelling collector doesn't stay long enough in any one place to have to worry about making lasting relationships. The rapport he establishes is relatively superficial or shallow. Casual trips into almost any bar, barbershop, hotel lobby, or bus station, where transient relationships are the rule, may result in the collection of considerable materials.[22] But should the collector attempt to do any depth collecting from such informants, he will have to establish rapport of a much deeper nature. Then, too, certain types of folklore materials are easier to collect than others under conditions of casual or momentary rapport. Storytellers, of various degrees of expertness, exist everywhere, and collecting from them can often be less formal. Song collecting, on the other hand, usually involves more patience, personality problems, and greater depth in

21. This is one of the ways in which a "passive" tradition bearer becomes an "active" one. See C. W. von Sydow, *Selected Papers on Folklore Published on the Occasion of his 70th Birthday* (Copenhagen, 1948), p. 15.

22. See, for example, Richard M. Dorson, *Bloodstoppers and Bearwalkers* (Cambridge, Mass., 1952). In his excellent introductory chapter, "The Background of this Book," pp. 1-12, Dorson describes the very casual and chance manner in which many of more than 1,000 tales were collected in a period of five months.

rapport establishment. And, too, some types of folklore involve such personal feelings and attitudes that casual rapport will not be sufficient to obtain them. The white collector who attempts to collect Negro tales may find that he will obtain generally innocuous material at the beginning, but that as the informant-collector relationship deepens, the tales recited may take on a very different hue indeed and involve protest items and race relations anecdotes. A Jewish collector working in a non-Jewish community may have to establish a very special relationship with his informants before they will tell him stories which they believe to be anti-Semitic or involving a stereotype of the Jew which may disturb the collector.[23] The collector must never lose sight of the fact that collecting involves a two-way relationship, with the informant frequently as solicitious for the collector as the collector is solicitous for the informant.

The collector whose project is of the order which creates many casual rapport relationships has one great advantage working for him: stranger value. The collector who comes from afar and will disappear again will be able to collect materials and information which might not be divulged to one who has a long-term residence in the same area.[24] The depth collector has this advantage, too, at the beginning of his field work, especially if he has not indicted how long he will be staying in the area. As his stay continues and he becomes less a stranger, he tends to lose this advantage and must devise other means (usually through the establishment of fundamentally deep relationships) for collecting materials of the type which he obtained when he still had his stranger value.

23. My own experience in collecting from a few Negro storytellers and many White singers and storytellers in North Carolina brought this point home to me very clearly.

24. Oesar, p. 410.

6. Maintaining Rapport

Once rapport is established, whether with the community in general or the individuals who are the collector's informants, the problem of rapport is not ended. The collector must maintain and continue to improve rapport. At any point in his relations, factors beyond his control may upset the balance, or his informants may simply lose interest in the collector and his work and show him less cooperation. There is no way of knowing when these will occur. When they do, the collector must face them, and find a solution if he is to continue working effectively.

The collector can, however, minimize the possibility of such occurrences by his attention to the problem of general rapport with the community. This can be achieved through the avenues of participation in the community's activities which are open to him. From the moment he enters the community he takes on many roles which are common to other persons in the community. He is involved in the problems of housing, transportation, medical services, and food and fuel supplies. In solving these problems, he has already begun a whole series of participation activities which he must continue and expand as long as he remains in the community. An examination of the various activities in which he may participate seems in order at this point, for they crucially involve the whole problem of rapport maintenance and in addition may help the collector to obtain answers to some of the folkloristic questions which inevitably arise in the field.

In obtaining housing, the collector will, in most cases, rent a house, share one with a citizen of the community, or move into a local inn or hotel. Any of these actions immediately sets up a series of personal relationships, the participants in which can assist the collector in learning the ways of the community and perhaps lead him to potential informants if they are themselves not active folklore bearers. In Strichen, Aberdeenshire, the house into which my family and I moved was owned by a woman who was extremely superstitious and who supplied us with a cross-section of the many beliefs held by the people of the community.

The collector will need household supplies and services of various kinds. Milkmen, firewood salesmen, coalmen, and others supplied us with their wares and choice bits of gossip, leads to informants, and interesting items of folklore as well. Our milkman, for example, when we rose early enough to meet him, would greet us with traditional weather prognostication rhymes and sayings.

Food supplies, hardware goods, and clothing should, when possible, be purchased from local merhants. Your business will be welcomed and you will have the opportunity to come into casual contact with other customers, near town gossip, and allow yourself to be sized-up by the local citizens. I met several of my best informants on queues in local greengrocer and butcher shops in Scotland, one of whom took me on visits to many of the leading traditional singers of the area.

When travelling from town to town or to wherever the local transportation system runs, the collector is well advised to use the same public transportation as do the local folk. The genial and casual companionship which usually results from such trips can be rewarding to the collector. I obtained 22 examples of folk cures for rheumatism from three fellow bus travellers who commiserated with my suffering from that affliction. On another occasion my wife met several fine traditional singers when she was caught in a train for 21 hours during a snowstorm; the passengers started singing to pass the time until snowplows were able to reach the train.

The collector may have recourse to use the local doctor, who frequently knows intimately most of the community's inhabitants, and may direct him to some potential informants. The doctor may possibly be acquainted with local folk remedies whose application usually precedes his being called on to treat some patient. Then, too, he is usually acquainted with the full medical history of any of his patients, some of whom may be the collector's informants. Since he is usually better educated than most local folk, he will be able to appreciate and understand the collector's work, and if convinced of his scientific and moral integrity, he may supply the collector with medical data which will help to complete the collector's picture of his informants. From a local doctor I was once able to obtain the medical reason for one of my informant's seemingly strange actions during certain of my visits to her. From then on I checked with the doctor so that I could coordinate my visits with her normal periods.

The role of the collector's wife (if he has one) has already been touched on slightly. Not only is she in an excellent position to socialize with local women and collect women's lore, but she is the entrée for the male collector into the private world of women's activities and gossip as well as to children's life in the community.

The collector who brings his children into the field is able to overcome the peer-transmission problems peculiar to children's lore. My own children acted as catalysts, bringing their young classmates from school into our home, directing collecting sessions with them for me and informing me which folklore materials were learned in the schoolroom and which were street or unsupervised playground traditions. Through these children I was able to arrange meetings with their parents when other contacts would have taken longer to arrange. As the parent of school children, I was invited to various school affairs, including dances and dinners, at which I was able to observe the manner in which local folk treat formal social functions in comparison with the informal social entertainments in which they took part at home.

Through similar local affairs, my wife and I were invited to join various local organizations. As a member of the Women's Rural Institute my wife learned about local ideas concerning poverty, charity, education, women's roles, folk recipes, and kitchen methods from women coming from a wide range of social, economic, and educational backgrounds. An invitation to join the local young farmers' group enabled me to study the changes that were going on in the traditional farming concepts in which superstition and belief were slowly being replaced by scientific farming and breeding techniques. Though I had never been a farmer, and certainly was not playing such a role in the community, the invitation was extended to me as a friendly gesture. Such an honor invariably carries some responsibilities with it, and I was asked to address the membership on my work in the area. In speaking before the group I talked of older farming traditions about which I had read, such as the Gudeman's Croft[25] and the Horseman's Word.[26] As a result of the speech I was later approached by several older farmers who were able to give me first-hand descriptions of these traditions from their own experiences, and finally led to my discovering that several of these farmers still kept Gudeman's Crofts.[27] Later, notices appeared in a local newspaper that I was to give a lecture at the local library on traditional singing illustrated by tape recordings of local folk; this drew a large crowd including, among the folk who were strangers to me, some who became new informants when visited in their own homes.

25. For references to the Gudeman's Croft, see Rev. Walter Gregor, *Notes on the Folk-Lore of the North-East of Scotland* (London, 1881), pp. 115-116, and J. M. McPherson, *Primitive Beliefs in the North-East of Scotland* (London, 1929), pp. 134-141.

26. For references to the Horseman's Word, see McPherson, pp. 290-1.

27. I have written of this in my article "Ghosts, Witches, and the Devil in Northeast Scotland," *Fulbright Courier*, March 1960, pp. 19-24.

With participation in full swing, the collector may find himself the recipient of numerous social invitations. These may be for local holiday meals, parties, and annual celebrations, and as guest of honor at calender custom events. To refuse any would be an insult, and the collector may be forced practically to cut himself into pieces to fufill overlapping invitations. When asked to be "first foot"[28] on Hogmanay Eve by three different families, each of which was several miles from the others, I was in a dilemma. Fortunately each of the three understood my problem and so two of them respected my tardiness in not showing up immediately after midnight for my ritual appearance and entrance. Later on I was to make the expected Hogmanay visit tour through the homes in the community in which I was living. In the process I consumed several pints of Scotch, and had an excellent chance to observe Scots drinking habits and consumption potentials, in addition to listening to lots of good singing and story-telling in a natural context, though by the time I returned to my own house at 6:00 the next morning, I was certainly in no condition to write up my notes on the experience with any degree of clear-headed objectivity.

Local public entertainment activities, such as dances and local amateur theatre musical shows, not only present the collector with additional opportunities for meeting people under genial conditions, but allow him to study and understand popular entertainment forms. At such times a collector is in a position to learn something of folk aesthetics. Though only an occasional informant will be able to supply critical value judgments on his own songs and stories, he will frequently be a strong and extremely vocal critic of the entertainment efforts of others, especially of those who are foolhardy enough to perform on stage.

28. For a description of "first footing" see: F. Marian McNeill, *The Silver Bough*, Vol. 3, *A Calendar of Scottish National Festivals* (Glasgow, 1961), pp. 104-106.

Informal socializing is one of the best means of rapport maintenance and will supply the collector with an opportunity to see his informant friends at ease. Afternoon or evening invitations to tea or coffee, with no pads, pencils, or recording machines in view, will help to cement feelings of comaraderie and set up joking relationships which can tell the collector more about the natural contexts of storytelling and singing than any formal field work could do. Exchange visits may lead to the collector throwing his home open as an informal gathering place for neighboring adults and children, and create an ideal atmosphere for informal interviewing and collecting.

Perhaps the most valuable avenue of participation which is open to the collector is for him to attempt to work with the local people in their normal occupational pursuits. His gesture at learning local skills, or of actually helping to augment the labor force when needed, will be greatly appreciated, even if his mechanical ineptness glares through. If the effort is made with genuine grace and a minimum of condescension, the gesture will aid in promoting good feelings. And it will again give the local folk a chance to play the role of instructor to the collector.[29] That such participation will also supply the collector with an opportunity to observe and listen to the normal traditions involved in the occupations of his informants can not be overestimated. Insights into occupational lore and the normal performance of folklore during working hours will assist the collector in understanding the context of such materials and supply him with informal interview opportunities during which he can explore certain lines of inquiry without the tenseness which might result from the same questions being asked outside the context of the work situation.

29. Paul, p. 436.

Not all contacts with informants are made through participation in the community's activities. Though a large number will, of course, come through introductions and leads supplied by non-performing folk whom the collector has met during the course of participation, some may have to be sought out by the collector using survey field methods. Many tradition bearers, especially passive ones, may not even be known as performers by their friends and neighbors. Visits to all the farms and rural households within a certain area may turn up some passive bearers from whom a collector may garner a fair amount of folklore. Occasionally, exceptional performers with extraordinary repertories who are not known for their talents by their fellow countrymen will be located by such a survey. Some traditional singers and storytellers are part of a private family tradition, and while these talented folk would never think of performing for local people, they may consent to perform for a friendly stranger. In the case of a community which has not previously been covered by field work, or where the field worker has neither the time nor the inclination to avail himself of the many avenues to leads which will come from participation, the survey may be the only road to finding the tradition bearers in a given area. Whatever the reason may be for the collector seeking informants without leads, there can be no greater thrill than to discover by one's own initiative an unusually fine folklore informant. And since most communities at this late date have at most only one or a few really talented traditional performers (if they have any at all) ,[30] the collector is indeed fortunate who makes even one such discovery on any field trip. For the field worker who can take advantage of participation, however, the road leading to most of his informants will be paved for him by one or another of his participant contacts.

30. Jansen, "From Field to Library," pp. 153-154.

7. Limitations and Hazards of Participation

No matter how much the field worker participates in the activities going on around him, he should always be aware that at best he can only partially penetrate the life of the community even under the most favorable circumstances. He comes into the community as a stranger and he will eventually leave as a stranger, albeit a much enlightened one.[31] His own eagerness to accept the inhabitants on their own terms does not mean that they will fully reciprocate in accepting the collector on his terms. Cautiousness toward strangers is a normal part of the tradition of most people. In some regions, even birth in the community does not entitle people to status as "natives." During the ten months of my stay in northeastern Scotland, I was to become aware of the fact that even a lifetime spent in the community would not change my status as "incomer."

Even with the establishment of rapport short of complete acceptance, the collector must be aware of other limitations to his participation in the community. Though he may consort with members of his own age and sex group at a level of equality, he must contend with lesser acceptance from other individuals in the community. To some degree this matter may be ameliorated by the presence of the collector's wife and children, who will extend the inclusion of the family into a wider range of sex and age groupings, but will still not begin to cover all of the many groups that exist.[32]

Even within those groups with which excellent rapport has been established, the collector is forced to respect the privacy of his informants on certain intimate matters. An

31. Paul, p. 437.
32. Ralph Piddington, *An Introduction to Social Anthropology*, Vol. II, (Edinburgh, 1957), pp. 548-549.

ill-advised attempt to invade this privacy may well result in a rebuke and the destruction of all the good will which he has worked to build up to that point.

The collector must also be aware of a fundamental fact: his very presence changes to some degree every situation in which he participates. Though full awareness of this fact will assist the collector in the objective evaluation of his data, it does not enable him to erase it as a factor. He participates as an outsider, which fact is an important element in interactive relationships with his informants. To obtain total naturalness in any social situation, the collector would be forced to remove himself wholly from the situation, thereby making it impossible for him to participate, observe or enquire. Even an experienced collector, utilizing the full range of techniques at his command, can at best only minimize his own effect on the situation.

Every community has some degree of hostile factionalism. Full participation in the community would necessitate the collector's taking sides. In certain circumstances this may serve part of the object of his investigation, but in all cases it will result in his own alienation from the opposing members. And, indeed, his taking sides may be viewed as interference by both sides and make it impossible for him to work further with either faction. The collector is seemingly obliged to remain neutral in such affairs, yet even there he is in danger of being caught in the crossfire.[33] The collector must weigh all factors carefully as they arise and make his decisions in the light of his problem objectives.

Perhaps the greatest limitation to the collector's participation in the community is the limited time at his disposal. His involvement in the affairs of the community serves to assist him in achieving the aims of his field work. He

33. Paul, p. 438.

must not, however, carry participation so far that he is unable to find the time necessary to carry out pertinent inquiry.

One of the hazards of participation is that the collector's desire to win good will may unwittingly lead him into enmity both with the persons toward whom his attentions are directed as well as those who become jealous of what they believe to be favoritism. As most Americans are aware from our international policies, even the best of intentions are often misconstrued. Favors must be given cautiously, with no strings attached and with no chance of the recipient being embarrassed. No fanfare should be attached to favor-granting; gossip concerning the act can then be kept to a minimum and the collector may be able to avoid any jealousy resulting from his good intentions.

In communities in which superstition reigns and understanding of cause and effect is minimal, the collector may find himself a scapegoat blamed for things with which he has nothing to do. When I was collecting in a mixed community of old Yankee families and Shinnecock Indians on Long Island, New York State, a case of poltergeist phenomena which occurred during the time of my field work was first blamed on the Indian members of the community and was then transferred to me as the only outsider there. No amount of denial or explanation on my part was able to soften the accruing hostility. The confession of two juvenile members of the community who had plotted and carried out the hoax came too late to exonerate me, as I had already abandoned my work there to collect in another part of the state. My lack of full participation in the community had boomeranged through my having formed few deep relationships, and no one there felt strongly enough to stand up for me. It is quite possible, however, that even if I had spent more time in participating in the community's activities and establishing rapport,

I would still have been blamed for the event merely because I was an intruder in the normal affairs of the
community.

In addition to the limitations and hazards of participation indicated above, the collector is also faced with the
possible costs to him of such participation. Primary among
these is personal discomfort. Under the strain of constantly
accommodating himself to others, of living in the public
spotlight, of having his good nature taken advantage of, of
playing a role and living up to the status it carries, of not
being able to indulge in his own idiosyncrasies while
forced to tolerate those of others, of continually being
careful to avoid untoward incidents and then having to
deal with them as they inevitably arise—under the strain
of all these and more the collector's patience is sure to be
strained. Emotional stability will only delay the strain.
His personal discomfort resulting therefrom must eventually affect his field work.

"Participation implies emotional involvement; observation requires detachment. It is a strain to try to sympathize
with others and at the same time strive for scientific objectivity."[34] If the collector over-identifies with his informants,
his scientific observation, evaluation, and anlysis may be
impaired. Aware of this possibility from his training, the
collector must continually evaluate his relationships with
the community and his informants in order to guard
against it. But just being on guard can itself result in
considerable discomfort.

There are several remedies for this participation fatigue.
One of these may be considered a preventive remedy: the
collector periodically reviews his degree of participation
and, according to his knowledge of his own personality
and of his physical and psychological endurance limits,
decides how much he will participate in the community's

34. Paul, p. 441.

affairs. By this means, assuming he has adequately assessed his own limits, he may indeed be able to avoid reaching the point of participation fatigue.

The second remedy is more mechanical (but perhaps more realistic) in that it simply involves the collector wholly removing himself from the field situation. This may be done by his taking off for a three- or four-day vacation each month, within easy travelling distance of, but totally removed from, the social scenery of the work area. Or the collector may simply wait for the first signs that his continued role-playing is beginning to affect his work and then take off until he feels that his equanimity has returned.[35]

In determining the degree to which he will participate in the community's activities, the collector must keep two sets of factors in mind: (1) active participation enables him to assuage suspicion, establish rapport, and enhance the naturalness of his position in the community, and (2) participation opens new avenues to understanding his informants and the community and should lead to the collection of more and better data to be used in problem solution.[36] Thus, in a very real sense, participation may be the key to successful field work.

35. The time away from the field can be used by the collector to review the data he has collected up to that point. The review may reveal blank spaces in the data and supply the collector with a guide as to the work needed to complete the project.

36. Marie Jahoda, Morton Deutsch, and Stuart W. Cook, *Research Methods in Social Relations*, Vol. I (New York, 1951), p. 142.

CHAPTER VI

Observation
Collecting Methods

OF THE SEVERAL METHODS AND TECHNIQUES which may be used by the collector in field work, two will serve to supply him with practically all the data necessary for the solution of field problems. These two methods—observation and interview—have been increasingly discussed by anthropologists, sociologists, and other social scientists, but rarely have they been commented upon the folklorists. It will therefore be necessary to define them for those folklorists who have not previously placed them in a conceptual framework of collecting theory.

Observation methods: Those methods used by the field worker in obtaining data by direct observation, looking from the outside in and describing the situation as he sees it. The term "observation," as used in this context, is not limited only to visual aspects of the situation, but also involves a full range of sensual experience including hearing, feeling, smelling, and tasting, whenever these may be appropriate.

Interview methods: Those methods used by the field worker to obtain data about ideas or events outside the context of the interview itself through questioning persons believed or known to have that information. During the interview, the informants describe situations, materials, attitudes, or ideas from the vantage point of the insider.

Ideally, a combination of both methods should yield the widest range of data. But the balance of emphasis on the use by the collector of one method or the other shifts with the frame of reference.[1] The collector wishing to describe a storytelling situation will probably prefer to view the situation himself, and may supplement such data by interviewing participants in order to obtain their ideas of what occurred. Conversely, the collector wishing to obtain the participants' aesthetic evaluation of a particular storytelling situation must depend mainly on interview methods, supplementing these by inferring the value system through observing the informants' actions and statements during the storytelling situation itself.

The two methods will be described in detail, together with an evaluation of their limitations and advantages, in this and the next chapter.

1. The Participant Observer

The field worker whose frame of reference calls for the direct observation of the actual context in which folklore exists may approach the situation from one of two possible vantage points. He may either play the role of an active participant in the situation to be observed, or he may merely be an onlooker or inactive participant.

1. Benjamin D. Paul, "Interview Techniques and Field Relationships" in *Anthropology Today*, ed. A. L. Kroeber (Chicago, 1953), p. 442.

As a participant observer[2] he will have many advantages working for him. If he is able to disguise his purpose and is accepted as an equal in the situation, he will be able to study the situation in as natural and unaffected a state as possible. In so doing not only will he be able to observe what goes on around him, but he will also be able to feel through experience the actual role which he assumes. As an active participant he is able to identify with other participants in the same role; he is thereby enabled to obtain information on the internal content of the situation instead of only its mechanics. Such information will give him a greater grasp of the situation, which in turn will assist him in formulating meaningful questions to be asked in follow-up interviews with other participants.

There is, however, one main disadvantage to assuming the role of participant observer. As a participant the collector will be unable to take notes during the situation itself, and must delay putting his impressions on paper until after the event is over. If the event is a long one, or has many participants or a large number of separate actions, it may be possible for him to retain only a portion of the many things that need to be remembered and recorded.

The ability of the collector to become a participant observer in folklore events is usually limited. Unless he has spent sufficient time in the community and has participated in many of its affairs, thereby achieving generalized acceptance, there is little chance of his being

2. The term *participant observer* will be used throughout this work to designate a fieldworker who participates in a *folklore* context or event which is being studied by him. It should not be confused with general participation in the activities of the community, except in so far as certain of those activities are folklore events. If the anthropologist's problem concerns the activities of a community, then every time he participates in any of its activities he does so as participant observer. The folklorist's problem concerns only the folklore activities of the community, and he is therefore a participant observer only when he participates in folklore activities.

able to participate without his presence being consciously noted by other participants; the very fact that his presence has been noted may change the naturalness of the situation to such a degree that an artificial situation is created. In some cases, he can never hope to attain generalized acceptance, especially if he is sufficiently physically differentiated from the local populace as to have a high degree of social visibility.

The collector may, however, observe many situations simply as an onlooker or inactive participant. In such situations he remains on the fringe of the action and notes the mechanics of the event. As a non-participant he may be able to view the situation with an objectivity of which participation would have robbed him. And as he is not in the center of the action he may be able to take notes, view the entire kaleidoscope of activities, and perhaps even be able to use a tape recorder to obtain a full report of the audio aspects of the event. His role of note-taking onlooker, however, may create self-consciousness in the participants to a degree which may radically affect the situation. In such cases, he is advised to cease his note-taking and to put his impressions on paper after the event is over.

2. Types of Contexts

Whether the observer role which the collector selects is that of a participant or of an onlooker, his main purpose in playing such a role is to observe and report on the context in which folklore exists or is performed. Such contexts have usually been considered on two levels: (1) natural folklore contexts, and (2) artificial folklore contexts. These can be described as follows:

1. *The Natural Context*: This is the social context in which folklore actually functions in a society.

Though there are several ways in which social situations can be classified for purposes of analysis (according to the number and types of participants, the kinds of behavior involved, the form and content of interaction, and so forth), the most useful classification system for the folklore observer involves the degree of formality of any context, for it is this factor more than any other which determines the manner and the degree to which the collector is permitted to carry out his observations. For reasons of convenience the formality of any context may be classified as (a) highly formal, (b) semi-formal, or (c) informal.[3] The *highly formal context* is one which is organized, required, and sometimes scheduled. Included in this group would be activities performed on special occasions, such as births, deaths, and weddings, or at specific times of the year, as calendar customs taking place at Halloween, Christmas, New Year. *Semi-formal contexts* are those in which folklore performance or statement is expected, but not required. Examples of this would include parents telling their children tales before sending them off to bed, a father reciting riddles to his child for educational purposes, or experienced cowhands spoofing a dude during his first days on a ranch. *Informal contexts* are those in which folklore is performed incidentally or casually, and in which such performance is not required, is unscheduled, and is usually unexpected (for example when an individual recites a proverb in the course of conversation, a man tells a joke to his barber while getting a haircut, or a farmer recites a weather-prognostication rhyme to a neighbor as the sun sets.)

3. The terms indicate a relative position on a scale, and are not absolute in any sense. For this reason there are likely to be contexts which may fit into the scale between any two contiguous points of the three given here. The collector should use his judgment as to which of the three ordinal points is closest to the context being classified.

2. *The Artificial Context*: This is the context in which folklore is performed to order at the instigation of the collector. Such a context is usually highly formal in that it is organized and scheduled by the mutual agreement of the collector and his informants.

The only truly natural context, of course, is one in which no collector is known to be present. Though performance of a folklore item will vary according to the pose requirements of the item, the function of the item in a particular situation, and the skills of the performer,[4] such performance in a natural context is, for the most part, unselfconscious. The intrusion of the collector into a folklore context changes the situation to one in which the actions and performances of the participants become self-conscious to some degree.

Of the two contexts—natural and artificial—the ideal one for recording folklore materials and observation data is the natural context. If the collector is able to observe a natural context, he can learn a great deal about folklore processes. First, he will be able to record behavior simultaneously with its spontaneous occurrence. Such observation will permit the collector to find out what people actually do rather than what they say they do. Second, observation may reveal data which informants take so much for granted that they would be unlikely to comment upon them in interview sessions. And third, since ideal observation conditions (in which the collector's presence is not known to the performer) do not require the informant's active cooperation, it is possible to obtain data independent of the subject's willingness to report them.[5]

4. William Hugh Jansen, "Classifying Performance in the Study of Verbal Folklore" in *Studies in Folklore in Honor of Stith Thompson*, ed. W. E. Richmond (Bloomington, 1957), pp. 110-118, discusses factors which may be taken into consideration when evaluating or classifying performance.
5. Marie Jahoda, Morton Deutsch, and Stuart W. Cook, *Research Methods in Social Relations* (New York, 1951), pp. 131-132.

There are, unfortunately, severe limits to the possibility of the collector's observing folklore performance in certain natural contexts. In the case of many *formal* natural contexts, the collector will have little difficulty in making his observation. In folklore events being watched by large numbers of spectators, he will have no difficulty in slipping into the audience with a minimal effect on the performers. And knowing when certain calendar customs take place, he can prepare adequately in advance to fit himself in as inconspicuously as possible. For certain other formal contexts, while he would probably have little difficulty in arranging to be an observer, the events might never occur during the collector's stay in the community. For example, a field worker interested in collecting burial or wedding lore may desire to observe such events, but unless a funeral or a wedding takes place during the period of his field work he may be forced to obtain his data by means of interviews with those in the community who have observed such events. There are, of course, certain events which collectors would rarely be permitted to observe, even if they should know when and where they will occur. Few collectors were ever permitted to observe the secret initiation rites of The Horseman's Word[6] in Scotland; most of the data we have is from interviews with and reminiscences of members of the organization. The affairs of certain sex- and age-oriented groups is also likely to be out of bounds to the collector. I was informed several times of obscene story- and song-sessions which would take place during women's tea parties at a specific place and time; unfortunately, my sex eliminated me as a potential participant or onlooker and I was forced to obtain my data about such sessions during interviews with one or more of its participants with whom I was on especially good terms.

6. See Chapter V, footnote 26.

The only problem in observing semi-formal contexts is getting permission to be present at them. If the collector has done a good job of establishing and maintaining rapport, he will usually be permitted to observe semi-formal folklore events if he happens to be present or can arrange to be present. Often, however, because the events are not scheduled, the collector may not be aware of them until the opportunity has passed.

Observing informal contexts is entirely a matter of accidentally being there when they occur. The more the collector participates generally in the activities of the community, the greater the number of such accidental occurrences it will be his fortune to observe or participate in.

The artificial context places fewer restrictions on the collector-observer. Since the time and place of the context are normally the common knowledge of both the observer and his informants, the collector is likely to utilize his time effectively for observation purposes. In the artificial context a performer can be asked to simulate performances which would otherwise be given in natural contexts, and if the natural context for such performance is one which has a specific type of audience, then the collector can attempt to duplicate audience factors as well. If the conditions of a natural context have been well duplicated, and the performer is relatively unaffected by the presence of the collector, it may be possible for a collector to successfully make observations which he might not have been able to make in a natural context. The collector can then concentrate on any facet of performance which specifically interests him and make detailed observations and recordings without worrying about the degree to which his presence might change the context.

There are, however, major shortcomings and limitations to artificial context observations. Only certain types of contexts can be duplicated by the artificial context, usually those with only a limited number of participants. Storytelling and singing contexts in which only one or two performers and a small family audience are involved can usually be duplicated, but larger functions cannot.

The greatest limitation to a collector making observations in artificial contexts lies not in his ability to duplicate natural contexts, but in his duplicating the unselfconsciouness of the the human elements in such contexts. Many, if not most, traditional performers cannot perform naturally in any context other than the real one. They are unable to play a part (no matter how familiar it may be to them) at the whim or order of a collector. For many informants the loss of situational familiarity and meaning is so great that they cannot perform effectively. One of my informants in northeasten Scotland could not recall his songs in an artificial context. Outside of his shoe repair shop he felt lost when attempting to sing his songs. I brought him his shoe-mending equipment and asked him to fix my shoes and sing his songs. The attempt was a failure. I took him at his word when he told me: "If ye come tac me shop, I'll fairly fill yer tape wi' song while I mend yer sheen there." In the natural context of singing while working in his own shop, he performed some thirty ballads without pause, hesitation, or memory loss; in the artificial context I was able to garner only imperfect and fragmentary texts and tunes. Needless to say, the only meaningful observations of his performance style worth reporting would be those made in the natural context of his shop.

Almost all collecting and most observations have been made in artificial contexts, probably because they impose fewer restrictions on the comfort of the collector. For the collector interested in obtaining only the materials of folklore, the context has never been much concern. The artificial context is usually the only one known to him. But even that handful of collectors who are interested in more than the materials, who are interested in documenting folklore processes and performance style—even these enlightened people have too often published their reports from observations made in artificial contexts. This is not to gainsay the reliability or objectivity of their observation reports. But unless a collector is sure that there is no appreciable difference between his informants' performances in artificial contexts and in natural contexts, then a report of observations made only in artifical situations may be almost worthless.

One of my Scots informants was a fine stylist both as a singer and as a storyteller. In natural contexts her performances never failed to hold her audiences spellbound. When performing in the artificial collector-informant context, she was able to retain a high degree of artistry in singing, but became a commonplace or even poor performer of tales. But even her song performances in the artificial context were not of the same order as her natural context performances of the same pieces. Her performance in the artificial context involved slower tempos and highly dramatic hand and body gestures and facial expressions, none of which were present to the same degree in her natural context performances. When asked to explain the differences in her performance style, she stated that since there was going to be a permanent record made of her performance she wanted to show herself at her best; and to her, her best meant "hamming-up" the performance. In the case of storytelling the difference was even more marked. During formal collector-informant sessions she became overly careful of her enunciation and grammar, resulting in stammering and a visible degree of nervousness, with a concomitant loss of effectiveness in her storytelling art. To have described her performance styles on the basis of the observations made in an artificial context would have been ridiculous, as well as doing an injustice to her great talents. My duty, obviously, is to describe her performance styles as observed in natural context; the artificial context was valuable only for obtaining the texts and tunes of the materials themselves.

3. The Induced Natural Context

For those who would study style of performance, it should be fairly obvious from the descriptions given above that the collector should report his observations made in the natural contexts in which folklore is performed. But how can he do so in the limited time at his disposal if he can never even be sure when these natural contexts will occur? The answer to the problem is that the collector must induce or create the natural context. This may seem a contradiction, for if a context is instigated by a collector it is no longer natural and should be considered an artificial context. However, the manner in which a collector instigates a context for performance will determine the degree to which that situation is natural.

The process described below will vary slightly depending upon the kind of folklore being performed, the degree of cooperation he obtains from his fellow instigators, and the number, age, sex, and attitudes of the participants. However, in the twenty instances in which I tested this method since I first designed it, it has never failed to create a near-natural context, and proved vastly superior to artificial contexts for recording data on context and performance styles.[7]

The method of *natural context induction* involves three separate steps. The first of these requires the collector to determine what the natural context or contexts are for the performance of any specific genre of folklore in the

7. I have used this method to induce natural contexts for the observation of singing, storytelling, and riddling sessions among adults, and marbles playing and singing game performances among children.

community in which he is doing his field work. This information may be obtained in two ways: either through actually having observed the natural contexts (in which case there is less reason for having to induce a natural context) , or by interviewing persons who have participated in such contexts, and then depending upon their verbal descriptions of the situation to decide what context is to be re-created.

After the natural context to be recreated has been decided upon, the collector proceeds to the second step. At this stage he must find an accomplice or, where the situation permits, be the instigator himself. Folklore exisits in a social situation involving numbers of people. The collector chooses his accomplice from that group of people who would normally be participants in the natural context being re-created. Ideally, that person should himself be a performer, but of the type which may be designated as average or typical, rather than a star performer (the aesthetic evaluation to be used in such a choice should be that of the community involved). The accomplice's major role is to bring about the context in which he and others will perform. This he achieves by calling together a group of his cronies or friends for an evening of story-telling, singing, riddling, or any other lore normally performed in such a context. And he must do so with as litte fanfare as possible and without informing the participants that the purpose of the session is to allow a collector to observe them in action. When the participants arrive at the place selected for the session (usually the home of one of them) , the collector is introduced casually as if he had dropped in unexpectedly (or it may be planned for him to actually arrive after the others have gathered). Preferably there should be no recording equipment present to inhibit the context.

Once the session starts, the collector can either observe as a participant or simply drop into the background, sitting on the fringe of the group where he may take notes on the situation. If a tape recorder is not being used for recording the materials of the session, the collector should indicate the pieces performed by means of a code system or some mnemonic device. He can later call on each of the participants individually to obtain the actual materials themselves in an artificial context or interview session.

Slight variations on the method may be applied when appropriate. If the collector has established excellent rapport with his informants and has spent sufficient time simply socializing with them on occasions, with no folklore being overtly collected, he may be able to eliminate the need for an accomplice. Having found out what the normal context for riddling was in northeastern Scotland, I invited six of my informants over for a social evening one Saturday night. When the moment seemed appropriate, I led the conversation in the direction of riddles and posed one that I had heard from an informant who was not present. I then took the role of a participant observer and was able to study the situation in depth during the two hours that the riddling session went on. In the meantime, my wife sat in the background and made notes on each of the riddles posed. Since there was usually five or six minutes between the time when a riddle was recited and the answer was given, she had sufficient time to write out each riddle and indicate the name of the poser. I made notes on my observations of the riddling context immediately after my informant friends left the house later that evening. By playing the role of the instigator, I was able to hide the real purpose of the evening from every one of the other participants, thereby assuring a more natural context.[8]

8. For a report of some of the riddling context data which I was able to obtain by the use of this method, see my article "Riddling Traditions in Northeastern Scotland," *JAF* 76 (1963), pp. 330-336.

I have also been able to avoid using accomplices from among the folk by having a member of my own family play that role on certain occasions. Wishing to observe marbles games in action as played by the children in the neighborhood, I had one of my daughters bring several of her schoolmates to our home so that I could observe them while they played on our rear lawn. Generally, such games were never played in the presence of adults because most of the home owners on the block were angered by the children digging holes in their lawns in order to play their marbles games. My daughter introduced her friends to me and asked if it was all right to play marbles. After I gave my permission, my daughter dug the hole for the game about 15 feet from where I was sitting (according to a pre-arranged plan), so that the game would be in full view to me. I busied myself pretending to be writing letters, but actually was taking notes on the situation.

The *induced natural context* method has its limitations. Those events which are of a calendar nature, which occur only when a specific situation calls for them (such as birth, death, or marriage), or to which a collector could not be a participant or onlooker because he lacks the qualifications—those events could not be simulated in an induced context. It can, however, be used successfully for almost any semi-formal event which occurs naturally in a community, and without the collector having to wait for it to occur. And it further insures that he will be at the event to conduct his observations.

In the order of effectiveness in observation collecting the induced context ranks closely behind the natural context and far ahead of the artificial context. One of the three contexts is either the best or the only condition for the observation of any folklore event. With experience the collector will know which of the three to use for any specific situation which he wishes to observe.

4. What to Observe

With all that goes on in any folklore context which the collector may wish to observe, there is a real problem of exactly what he should observe. Ideally, if the collector wishes to "supply the greatest amount of reliable information to the largest number of potential users of such information," then he must observe and report on everything which goes on in the particular contexts at which he finds himself present. This is obviously impossible. "He cannot be everywhere at the same time, and he can never be sensitive to literally everything that occurs even within his field of view, much less record it all in its manifest complexity . . ."[9] He is expected, however, to note whatever is pertinent to his problem. To assist the collector in making his decisions of what to observe, I have compiled the list below. As far as I have been able to ascertain from my own field work experience, it covers most of the possible matters which a collector can observe and which may prove useful in answering the needs of folklore theory and practice:

1. *THE PHYSICAL SETTING*: INDOORS: The location of the house or other building in which the context occurs; size and shape of room used; adornments of the room (pictures, religious or other symbols, heating outlets, curtains and furniture); number and type of windows; amount and type of lighting; type of heating used and temperature; unusual sounds (such as bird noises, farmyard sounds, automobile or train noises) or the lack of them; unusual odors (cooking smells, animal odors, tobacco odors, and incense). OUTDOORS: Location; scenic layout; weather conditions; temperature; sounds; smells.

9. Paul, p. 442.

2. *THE SOCIAL SETTING*: For the persons present the following data should be obtained: number; sex; age; names; status in community; role and status in the existing folklore context; relationship of individuals to each other; placement or position in the physical setting; general appearance and dress.

3. *INTERACTION BETWEEN PARTICIPANTS*: Initiator of action; special roles in interaction; personal incentives; methods of encouragement or disapproval as shouts, applause, and footstamping; conflict actions (conversation while performance is taking place, separate performances going on at the same time, and other interruptions); rapport or empathy actions like shushing noise makers, or joining in with performers.

4. *PERFORMANCE*:   Introductory   commentary; style of performer (intonation, voice rhythm, continuity, speaking rate, pitch, vocal intensity, pauses, facial expressions, gestures, pantomime, voice imitation of characters or objects, repetition, and interjections); closing commentary; position and attitude of body; essential equipment (e.g., instruments for musicians) ; supplemental equipment (e.g., guitar used to accompany singer, noisemakers used by storyteller) ; deviations from normal performance (must be based on observer's prior experiences with performer or on comments from other observers) .

5. *TIME AND DURATION*: Time of day when situation begins and ends; time devoted to introductions, performance, intermissions, and socializing; duration of individual performances; exact order in which items are performed; time and duration of unusual occurrences (interruptions, illnesses of performers or members of audience, etc.) .

6. *SENTIMENTS EXPRESSED*: Verbal statements of approval or disapproval; verbal statements involving aesthetics (comments on quality of performance) ; emotional sentiments expressed (laughing, crying, etc.) .

7. *MISCELLANEOUS OBSERVATION*: Occasion for performance; manner in which participants were brought together; availability of food and drink; anything else which collector may feel pertinent.

8. *THE OBSERVER*: Observer's role in context; position of observer; observer's state of mind; observer's physical condition; factors contributing to observer's comfort or discomfort; events affecting observer.[10]

The above list may seem formidable. It is suggested that the observer first analyze his problem as it relates to the context being observed and then examine the above list to determine in advance which factors are likely to be pertinent to the problem's solution. The collector will then pay greater attention to those factors, and supplement such observations with whatever is pertinent that occurs during the situation.

5. How and When to Record Observations

The context being observed will usually be the main determinant as to when and how to record observations. Ideally, the collector should record his observations on the spot as he makes them; this will result in a minimum of

10. The category "The Observer" was suggested by comments made by Margaret Mead in "Problems of Process: Methods," *An Appraisal of Anthropology Today*, ed. Sol Tax, Loren Eiseley, Irving Rouse, and Carl Voegelin (Chicago, 1953), pp. 87-88.

selective bias and memory distortion. However, note-taking at an event is not always feasible. In the first place, it may interfere with the quality of the collector's observations, and writing notes takes time and attention—time and attention which would perhaps be better expended in continuous observation of the event; in the second place, and perhaps even more important in terms of the situation itself, note-taking may so disturb the naturalness of the context as to change its content and form. This last point, however, generally will not apply in artifiical contexts in which the collector's intentions and actions are known and manifest.

Where the collector has decided to make his observations as a participant in an event, note-taking is practically out of the question. Where he is merely an onlooker, he may be able to situate himself sufficiently outside the central action as to be able to take a few notes, to be augmented later; but because memory retention is the major factor, the recording of data should take place immediately after the event.

In observing a natural folklore context, the collector is rarely able to take down the materials performed therein unless they happen to be short pieces such as riddles, rhymes, or proverbs. The recording of longer pieces will have to be made during artificial, informant-collector sessions after the event itself. Before conducting such a session, the collector is advised to allow at least several days to pass between the natural context performance and the artificial context performance. In experiments with many of my own informants I have found that repetitions of folklore materials tended to be less effective (as performances) if such repetition took place within a short time after the initial performance. For example, in the case of tales, the repeated items tend to be shorter, less detailed, with performance style less dramatic. One of my informants explained such difference with the remark: "Ye've heard it afore an' I widnae be wastin' yer time wi' the hale bit o'er again." There is also the possibility that the thrill of performance is less keen at the time of repetition. The collector should experiment with his informants, having them repeat items at different intervals in order to determine the "forgetting time" for each informant. This did not apply to those of my informants who are professionals in the eyes of their countrymen. Such people could repeat tales again and again without any appreciable loss. The collector, however, should find out whether the situation described here exists for his informants, and allow for it accordingly.

In taking notes during an event or in recording details after the event, the collector must be careful to distinguish between observation and interpretation. In recording observation the collector is supposed to be describing the objective, factual situation. In actuality, however, only the observation itself can be objective; once the collector sets his pen to paper an element of interpretation is bound to creep in. Since a collector is incapable of reporting everything that he has seen, what he actually reports is a selection (consciously or unconsciously made) of the observable phenomena. Selection is in itself a factor of interpretation; and when one adds to this the bias which may result from the collector's temperament and outlook, among other unmeasurable factors which may crucially influence selection, one becomes aware of the immense problem in trying to distinguish between interpretation and observation.

Training in the logic of scientific methods will assist the collector with at least a partial solution of this problem; his very awareness of the problem is itself an important first step to minimizing error in this respect. In recording observations, the collector must attempt to eliminate at least the conscious elements of interpretation. A re-reading of the first drafts of observation reports should be made specifically for the purpose of separating observation from interpretation. Interpretation is part of a later stage of inquiry, and though it may be done in the field, the collector is wise to keep his interpretive notes separate from, or at least marginal to, his observation notes.

There are, to be sure, several ways in which limited controls and checks can be applied to the collector's observations. The first of these is the use of follow-up interviews with participants. Their familiarity with the situation may help to fill in details omitted by the collector as well as correcting his faulty impressions. The second is the use of additional personnel for the purpose of making simultaneous observations of the same event by different observers. The collector may be able to call on his wife or a local resident to record independent observations of an event which may include points which the collector's selective bias caused to be omitted. The value of the observations made by these supplemental personnel will depend upon the quality of their training, their objectivity, sensitivity, and intelligence. It is unlikely that the collector will have enough time in the field to adequately train local personnel to assist him in his work. The ideal situation would be to have husband-and-wife collector teams in which both parties have been trained in folklore theory and practice. Though there are and have been several such outstanding combinations among anthropologists, thre are unfortunately few among non-anthropological folklorists.[11]

6. Equipment as Observation Tools

As has been stated earlier, the ideal observation method would be one which would permit the field worker "to

11. For example, Frances and Melville J. Herskovits among anthropologists, and Alta and Austin Fife among non-anthropological folklorists.

observe and report on everything which goes on in the particular contexts at which he finds himself present." In actual fact, however, the folklorist has rarely called on the only piece of equipment, the sound camera, which could help him to come as close to the ideal as possible. With the sound camera the collector could obtain a record of events which would be more complete, accurate, and objective than could be obtained by any other means, and enable him to review the events for maximum understanding.

Some excellent sound films have been made of such formal folklore events as Mummers' fetes and folk dance competitions. A few have been made of folk-song artists, like Leadbelly and Jean Ritchie, but such artists achieved professional status as performers before the films were made; it is questionable whether many non-professional traditional performers could retain before the camera the unselfconsciousness which is a hallmark of their art. Unfortunately the few films of folklore content which do exist do not always serve to further folklore studies, mainly because they were produced by non-folklorists for the edification and entertainment of non-folklorist audiences.

There are several reasons for this poor state of affairs. High-quality sound photographic equipment is expensive. Also, too few folklorists are sufficiently interested in this technique even to care to learn how to use the sound camera with any degree of proficiency. But the most important factor militating against the use of the sound camera is one which is inherent in most natural folklore contexts—the difficulty of observing natural contexts without radically affecting them by the collector's presence. To attempt to use cumbersome equipment in such contexts would only multiply that difficulty. Ideally, such equipment would have to be out of the view of the persons and events being photographed. I have no knowledge of a folklorist planting secret equipment in order to record or film a natural folklore context.

John Ball has indicated how helpful a sound film library of well-told tales would be to the study of that genre of folklore.[12] The same need is felt in every other genre. The possibility of making such films in unaffected natural contexts is so slight that we need not discuss it further here. Nevertheless, the sound camera can be used effectively in observing certain artificial folklore contexts. Not all folklore performers are inhibited by the use of mechanical equipment; in fact, a few informants with whom I have worked have responded positively to it. The fact that their performances were being recorded seemed to have no effect on their performance style. By experimenting with his best informants, the collector may occasionally locate performers whose style remains relatively unaffected by the intrusion of this element. The collector must be sure not only that the presence and use of the equipment will not affect his informant negatively, resulting in a poor performance, but also it will not overly stimulate him and result in his "hamming-up" the performance.[13] When the collector locates star performers who remain unaffected by the presence of equipment, he should do everything possible to have these persons recorded on sound film. Perhaps some foundation would award a grant for such purposes; the result could be more important to folklore studies than several grants given for other field work projects.

12. John Ball, "Style in the Folktale," *Folk-Lore* 65 (1945), p. 171.

13. Some informants have several distinct performance styles, each of which is used for a different type of natural context. For example, a traditional Negro folksinger from whom I have collected performed almost offhandedly when singing in his kitchen for his own family and friends, and very animatedly when singing before street audiences for money. Both these contexts were natural for that particular singer. When singing for me in an artificial context, he assumed the pose which was natural to him for street singing sessions. A report of this informant's performance style should properly include descriptions of both styles and should not be limited only to the one observed in an artificial context.

Though less cumbersome, the motion picture camera without sound attachments has most of the same limitations for the filming of natural folklore contexts. Before motion picture equipment can be used effectively for recording natural folklore contexts, the camera industry will have to produce equipment no larger than hand size and film which is fast enough to be used in the most unfavorable lighting conditions.

Certain equipment has, of course, been used effectively in observational field work. Photographic stills of traditional singers and storytellers can be found in many collections published during the past 35 years. Although they are usually posed pictures, without the slightest sense of action in them, they do at least supply us with an idea of some of the human physical factors inherent in folklore; and they do help to add a dimension of human reality to the lifeless form of printed texts and tunes.

Though rarely used for such purposes, the still camera can be used by the imaginative collector for filming performance contexts. The collector-photographer who knows his equipment well can take whole rolls of film shots in rapid succession.[14] I have taken numerous shots of folksingers and storytellers in this manner which, in the absence of moving pictures, supplied me with the next best thing to action shots. These photos show changes in position, gestures, and facial expressions, all of which are important visual factors of style in the performance of folklore.

Certainly the most valuable piece of equipment in wide use in the field at the present time is the sound-recording machine. Since its first use by Jesse Fewkes in recording folklore texts and music of the Passamaquoddy Indians of

14. Photographers who wind their own rolls of film are able to take more than 40 shots on a single roll, depending, of course, upon the film size and type of camera.

Maine in 1889, the sound recorder (whether cylinder, disc, wire or tape) has proved an indispensable aid to ethnographers and musicologists in obtaining recordings of folklore materials studied by their respective disciplines.[15]

Folklorists, too, have used the machine mainly for recordings of folklore materials, rarely making use of it in observation field work. This is not surprising, since, until fairly recently, most western folklorists concentrated their studies on the materials rather than the processes of folklore; but even those folklorists interested in studying processes do no appear to have used the machine for other than interview purposes in addition to the recording of materials.

As a tool for observation field work, the recording machine plays the role of an auditor, supplementing the collector's role as a visual observer. It allows the collector to concentrate his observation activities on seeing, smelling, tasting and feeling, with less attenion having to be paid to aspects of sound which, for most contexts, is second in importance only to sight. Since the machine records the full range of sounds in the context, including the materials performed therein, the note-taking collector can concentrate his notes on other aspects. Indeed, it permits him greater freedom to play the role of participant observer (rather than that of onlooker), giving him a greater grasp of the internal feel of the context; and, too, the collector can effectively use the recordings made in context as a mnemonic device for recall when he writes his observations of the event.

The description given above for the use of the recording machine as a supplementary observer is an ideal one; in practice there are limitations to its use. Some machines

15. John Howland Rowe, "Technical Aids in Anthropology: A Historical Survey" in *Anthropology Today*, ed. A. L. Kroeber (Chicago, 1953), p. 914.

are bulky or dependent on an outside power source. These machines and their attendance would be an additional intrusion into a natural folklore context, causing some change in the context itself. Changing reels of tape in the case of long events, setting and changing sound levels, checking the power source—all these require the attention of the collector, thereby detracting from his observation activities. This, however, may be remedied by having the machine run by one of the local folk, a student, colleague, technician, or by the collector's wife. The ideal recording equipment would be compact and capable of making high fidelity recordings at low speeds, would be run by its own power pack, and would record sound through the medium of a professional quality wrist or lapel microphone. The collector can then set the machine at a single sound level at the beginning of the event and forget about it while he makes his observations, undisturbed by the needs of the machine.

The sound-recording machine plays all the above roles in artificial context observations as well. Its limitations on such occasions are less than for natural contexts.

A relatively inexperienced collector's early visits to an informant should be without equipment of any kind. After he has obtained permission to bring the equipment, he can introduce the machine into the collecting context. Having observed the informant during previous visits and having a base on which to make comparison, the collector can decide to what degree the presence of the machine and himself affects the informant's performance. If they change the performance style significantly, the collector should make his observations without the machine and use it only in the artificial context for obtaining materials.

An experienced collector, on the other hand, should be able to use the recording machine to good advantage from the first meeting with an informant. The machine should be almost inseparable from the personality of the collector, and he should be able to use it so unobtrusively that it will not affect the unselfconsciousness of the informant any more than would the collector's presence without the machine. Alan Lomax, who has probably used recording machines more often and to better advantage than any other American folklore field worker, feels that in a properly conducted first meeting with an informant the collector has an opportunity to obtain a peak of communication with his informant which may not be repeated until much later in their relationship:

> He [the informant] calls upon all of his emotional resources and sums up himself and his artistry very often in the first interview . . . and he will seldom repeat the concentration of energy and communication. City people are bothered by recording machines; country folk are not. Indeed, they often regard them as the only chance they have to make statements to the bigger world that they know about, which is always speaking to them and to which they never have an opportunity to reply. This, of course, is especially true of the star performers in the community, who are eager to join the communication system. Socially, our first function is to make them participants in this communication system.
>
> (Personal communication, October 6, 1963)

The recording machine may also serve the collector as a secretary-stenographer when he reports his impressions of a folklore situation or context. As soon after such a session as is possible, the collector can verbalize his observations into the microphone of the tape recorder, thus giving him a permanent record of his immediate impressions unhampered by the self-consciousness accruing from the hand-mind combination involved in writing out his impressions in long-hand or by typewriter. These recordings can be played back later when the collector is not restricted by the time limitations of the field, and his notes can then be transcribed to paper.

CHAPTER VII

Interview
Collecting Methods

INTERVIEWING IS THE MOST COMMON FIELD METHOD employed by folklore collectors. Interview data may include information on what the informant knows, believes, expects, feels, wants, does, or has done, or which explains or gives reasons for any of the preceding. It supplies the collector with an insider's view to the individual, his culture, and his folklore. And it also is the chief means of supplying the collector with the folklore materials themselves.

The previous chapter indicated that interviewing is a less direct way of obtaining certain information than is observation. The information which may be obtained through observation by the collector is limited to situations and performances which are external to the inner man; but in so far as the informant's feeling and judgments are concerned, interviewing is as direct a means of obtaining information as any other, and frequently it is the only means to obtain such information. Though the interview situation may be an artificial one for observing performance, it is at the same time practically the only natural context for eliciting information from an informant. A certain amount of such information may be inferentially obtained; but, since inference involves a considerable amount of interpretation, it is less to be preferred as a field method than interviewing.

Certain information can be obtained from an informant by directly soliciting it from him or from someone who knows him well. This would include the minimum vital data on an informant: name, age, residence, occupation, and where, when, and from whom he obtained the materials which he is passing on to the collector. Too often, however, such information is not viewed as minimal, but is all the information that the collector obtains because for most folklorists the materials themselves are the objective of field work. The process of folklore and the informants themselves are usually ignored. Yet at this point in folklore studies there is still much information which has not been sufficiently documented to be able to place those materials in a meaningful context. The folklorist must also concern himself with larger considerations if he is to know anything about the very essence of the materials which he studies. Questions involving the who, why, and how of folklore are as important as what, when and where.

1. Types of Interview Data

It is not the purpose of this book to serve as a listing of all the many problems to which field workers may obtain answers by the use of interview techniques, nor to indicate why it is important for folklorists to obtain the answers to such questions; that must come from their training in theory. Rather, its purpose is to indicate which interview methods can be used to obtain those

ᴇ doing so, however, it seems appropriate
ᴐ give examples of the several kinds of
cannot be answered by observation field
which interview methods and techniques
⸻ ᴛne best if not the only way to obtain
answers.

Basically, interview methods can be and are used to
obtain answers to the following kinds of questions:

1. *Personal history of informants*: Folklore materials
are human products, and a knowledge of the human
sources of folklore is being stressed more and more in
modern folklore scholarship. We want to know what
kind of person becomes a tradition bearer. What
are the forces which contributed to his becoming a
tradition bearer? In what way and why is he like or
different from other tradition bearers or from *non-
tradition bearers*?

2. *Aesthetics of Informants*: All art is created or performed in terms of an aesthetic, whether that aesthetic
is the result of conscious or unconscious thinking.
Much folklore is artistic in form and therefore
aesthetic. We want to know what feelings and judgments make up this aesthetic. Why do informants
perform certain pieces and not others? When they
have heard several variants of the same piece, why do
they perform one and not the others? What is a
"good" song or story, and what is a "bad" one? Who
is a "good" performer and who is a "bad" one? And
why are they good or bad?

3. *Knowledge, feelings, and meanings*: The functioning of folklore in a society presupposes not only an
aesthetic, but a series of ideas involving the informant's knowledge and attitudes, and the meaning which
the folklore materials have for him. Does an informant

have his own generic classification for the items in his repertory? What is the meaning to an informant of a specific item of folklore? What emotions does it evoke? If it is narrative, does the informant know the incident which it describes? Does he believe it to be true or false, and why? Of the many superstitions that an informant knows or has heard, why does he believe some and reject others? What does he think about or feel while he performs? Why does he remember certain items and forget others? What factors contribute to the remembering process? What effect do various kinds of audiences have on the performer?

4. *The transmission of folklore materials*: The transmission processes of folklore are still largely undocumented, and such data can only be obtained in the field. When, where, and from whom did the informant learn the pieces in his repertory? How were they learned? What were the circumstances of the first hearing of any particular piece and how often has it been heard since? How often does the informant perform that piece and under what circumstances? Has the informant made any changes in the materials in his repertory? How, and why? Does the informant have more than one way of performing any items?

5. *Descriptions of folklore situations which the collector is unable to observe*: Folklorists are as interested in folklore of the past as of the present for the two together give them an opportunity to study the forces of change. And they are equally interested in the many modern folklore situations and materials which they are unable to observe. What is the informant's report of activities at folklore situations at which the collector was not present? What kinds

of contexts existed in the past for folklore performance? In what ways have performance styles and
repertories changed through the years? Who were
the major performers in the community at an earlier
time?

6. *Informants' Repertories*: The interview situation
is usually the best or only context in which a collector
can obtain most of the longer folklore items in an
informant's repertory. Through the use of finding
lists or questionnaires, it also permits him to obtain
most shorter items as well, which otherwise could be
obtained only by being with informants for long
periods.

2. Interview Methods

Through their widespread use by many social research
groups, interviewing techniques have been refined and
perfected to the point where there exists a long list of
minutely defined variations on two basic methods.[1] For
the purpose of folklore field work a description of these
two methods should suffice, with the field worker encouraged to work out any variations or combinations
which his specific field conditions may call for.

The *non-directive interview* consists of a rather generalized conversation between a collector and his informant
in which the informant is allowed almost completely free
rein after the collector has suggested a subject. The collector is expected to keep his informant talking without
disturbing his thought processes and without unduly
influencing the informant's behavior or statements by
comments or by the force of the collector's personality.

1. For example, open-end, poll type, structured, non-structured, focused,
directive, non-directive, expressive, etc.

People like to talk about the things which interest them, and the field worker must be ready to appear interested in the same things. When the informant pauses, the collector must restrain himself from rushing in with a question. The hesitation may simply be a call for encouragement or recognition. This the collector may do by rewording or repeating something which the informant has just stated, by asking a neutral question, or simply by nodding his head—whichever may seem most appropriate at the moment. If the informant makes a statement which is either unclear to the collector or on which he wants further elaboration, the collector may indicate this by repeating the informant's words (with a question mark at the end), or by referring back to the matter when the speaker pauses for a moment. When the informant appears to have reached the end of his exposition, the collector may call a halt or begin the process over again by suggesting a new topic. The method encourages the informant's spontaneous responses as full and detailed as he is able to or cares to make them. It allows for a wide range of subjects and materials to be covered according to the informant's own manner of ordering them. By eliciting the personal and social context of beliefs and feelings, it serves to uncover the affective and value-laden implications of the informant's thinking.[2] This method is especially valuable in the earlier phases of rapport establishment because of its seeming casualness and lack of directed probing into the informant's life. At the same time, it may serve to uncover information which an informant would be unwilling to reveal in response to a direct question. By allowing his informant to ramble, the collector may stumble upon some facts or items of folklore which a more directed line of inquiry would never have disclosed.

2. Marie Jahoda, Morton Deutsch, and Stuart Cook, *Research Methods in Social Relations* (New York, 1951), Vol. 1, p. 175.

Once the collector has achieved some level of rapport with his informant, the *directive interview* may be employed. By a pointed series of questions the collector elicits highly specific information on particular subjects ideas, or materials. In most cases it is better actually to prepare specific questions in advance, with each question so ordered as to set up a frame of reference for succeeding questions. Though the questions may be prepared in advance, the collector is advised not to read them stiffly to his informant; he should be familiar enough with them to be able to ask them conversationally, preferably without the aid of notes. Though ideally the collector would like to be able to control the order of both the questions and responses, he must allow the interview to remain sufficiently flexible so that he can probe further into unanticipated avenues and directions, re-ordering questions when necessary or omitting some of them completely. The informant should be free to express his own ideas in his own terms and frame of reference, while at the same time the collector should discourage irrelevant conversation and endeavor to confine the informant to the discussion of the specific issues about which the collector seeks knowledge. The task is not an easy one, for the collector must be able to obtain the full cooperation of his subject in an atmosphere less permissive than that of the non-directive interview. The direction of the interview must always remain clearly in the hands of the collector without his ever directing the informant to one rather than another response. The informant must always feel free to express himself without fear of disapproval, admonition, or dispute. The skillful interviewer must be able to hide surprise, swallow laughter, and conceal boredom whenever an informants' responses kindle such emotions.

In actual use most interviews will consist of a compromise between the two techniques described, with the collector shuttling back and forth between them. A topic will be suggested and the informant will be allowed to ramble at first. At some point of special interest to the collector, the directive approach will be applied so that the conversation and responses may be kept within certain limits. The degree of compromise between the two methods will depend largely upon the kind of information being elicited.

Though no absolute rule can be set, the collector should be aware that posing a direct question may be an invitation to being given a distorted answer.[3] Rather than reveal his lack of understanding, an informant may simply answer "yes" to a direct question in the hope that the collector will go on to another question. But in the social context of the interview situation the collector is in a position to watch his informant's reactions, which may indicate his ability to comprehend what is being asked. At the slightest indication that a question has not been fully understood, or that it has been misinterpreted, the collector can reword the question in an attempt to find the informant's comprehension level.

Though the interview places heavy reliance on a verbal report when information is desired on the unobservable feelings, attitudes, value judgments, etc. of an informant, the collector must recognize that many people are unable to verbalize such things. "Many of our most important beliefs and motivations are inaccessible or unconscious; not being aware of them, we cannot report them."[4] Feelings, beliefs, and motivations become apparent to a person in an intellectually comprehensible form for verbal expression only at the end of a complex process of inference. Many people have never learned to make the inferences

3. Melville J. Herskovits, "Some Problems of Method in Ethnography" in *Method and Perspective in Anthropology*, ed. Robert F. Spencer (Minneapolis, 1954), p. 13.

4. Jahoda et al., p. 154.

necessary for an adequate verbal report,[5] but this fact should not hinder the collector from asking questions. Even partial answers may supply important data; and occasionally the collector will find that some of his informants have done quite a bit of self-analysis and are capable of answering almost any question. Indeed, the best performers are usually superior to the rest of the community in self-knowledge, sensitivity, and intelligence. And for those informants who seem incapable of self-analysis, the collector may be able to impersonalize his questions. Though unable to delve into the aesthetic judgments involved in an informant's choice of his own performance materials, the collector may be able to obtain some idea of that aesthetic by asking the informant to comment upon someone else's performance. The collector may do this by playing recordings of other informants or of commercially available recordings (in the case of songs). Many traditional performers have very strong ideas about other people's performances and repertories, and where they are unable to comment on their own they will attack others with a vengeance. Sometimes it will take a very direct remark by the collector to set off an informant's commentary. I informed one of my Scots informants that I had obtained from another singer a 52 stanza version of a ballad which she had given to me in only 14 stanzas. She quickly informed me that "Ye canna judge a song by the length o't. It's the story that coonts an' ye ken that my wye for it's nae waurse than the ither. Geordie's wye jist tak's a bit longer tae tell. An' I ken the hale o'it tee." And to prove her point she proceeded to sing a 50 stanza version of the same ballad!

3. Checking Interview Data

Even when he is able to obtain answers to all of his questions, the collector must not allow himself to be

5. Jahoda et *al.*, pp. 154-155.

deluded into believing that he has obtained truthful responses in every case. Sometimes informants will use their verbal replies to ingratiate themselves with a collector, or to gain his respect or the prestige of the community. Sometimes their answers are intended to amuse or to astonish the collector, or to create social effects which they find pleasureful or advantageous. Nor should the collector take at face value any statements which place informants in a favorable light when there is a suspicion that truthful answers might embarrass, humiliate, or degrade them.[6]

There are usually several avenues open to the collector by which he may check the verity of interview responses. Where the informant has given information relative to observable phenomena, the collector may check those statements by attempting to view the same or similar contexts. Generally it is a good rule, whenever possible, to supplement interview data with observation, and vice versa, whatever the frame of reference may be. The two methods frequently present different sides of the same coin.

A second check method is to conduct interviews on the same subject with other informants. Not only will this give the collector a chance to cross-check the honesty or accuracy of different informants, but usually it will also produce additional information.[7]

A third check is to conduct several interviews on the same subject with the same informant. This approach will serve three purposes: (1) It may be used to detect inconsistencies in information obtained in an earlier interview. Few indeed are the persons capable of lying and maintaining internal consistencies in their lies over several interviews. One of my informants kept lying about her background in order to hide the fact that she was a

6. Jahoda et al., p. 154.
7. Ralph Piddington, An Introduction to Social Anthropology, Vol. 2 (Edinburgh, 1957), p. 553.

member of a generally despised minority subgroup; several interviews revealed a number of startling inconsistencies. When I believed I had established excellent rapport with the family and could face them with my knowledge of their lying without greatly affecting our relationship, I proceeded to do so. She then admitted her attempted deception and corrected the previously distorted parts of the family history. Further checking by repeated interviews with her, with others in the same family and with outsiders proved the reliability of her corrected version. (2) Repeated interviews will help the collector to obtain a clearer impression of the matter being discussed. Descriptions by an informant of complex situations and feelings may be fitted together from several interviews, each of which contributes additional information to the whole. (3) The collector may use repeated interviews with the same informant to develop different aspects of the same question. For example, a first interview may be directed towards obtaining a description of the physical mechanics of a certain folklore context, a second toward its internal content, and a third towards a description of the historical changes which have taken place in the context during the lifetime of the informant.

Interviews with different informants on the same subject may result in different descriptions being obtained, without any element of lying entering into an explanation of the discrepancies. These may result from inherent differeces in points of view, in intellect and personality, and in the various levels of knowledge which different persons have.[8] Certain individuals in a community are bound to have more highly specialized knowledge of specific events than others: a baker, for example, can be expected to have knowledge of a wider range of beliefs and customs

8. S. F. Nadel, "The Interview Technique in Social Anthropology" in *The Study of Society,* ed. F. Bartlett et al. (London, 1939), p. 319.

relating to his occupation than would other members of a community. Some informants may be reluctant to part with their specialized knowledge to an outsider even after excellent rapport has been established. Usually an indication by the collector that he already has certain knowledge of the point under consideration may be used to draw out the informant at hand. The simple statement, "I've been told that this is the way that such and such is done," may result in an informant correcting, or adding to, the information which the collector already has.

4. Social Context of Interview Situations

Statements made by an informant may differ radically according to the social context of the interview situation. When he is alone with the collector, an informant may be willing to discuss things which he would never reveal in the presence of his neighbors or relatives. Then, too, informants may actually be restrained by their family or friends from making revelations which they believe may be harmful to them. The family of one of my informants refused to let her tell me about the "witch" in the town in the fear that such knowledge on my part would be traced back to them and might result in a curse being placed on them. When I had the informant alone, her gregarious nature and my promise that such information would never go past my notebook resulted in her spilling the whole story. By judicious interviewing of others in the community, I was able to establish the degree to which this belief pervaded the community and gained valuable data on the nature of witchcraft and of devil beliefs in the region.

The nature of an audience may greatly affect an informant's choice of words and subject matter. In the company of children, an informant who is especially proud of his knowledge of erotica may become reserved. Conversely, a normally taciturn New Englander may become loquacious when he is in the company of someone whom he wishes to impress. With a knowledge that the social context affects an interview situation, the collector may wish to conduct experiments to ascertain whether certain patterns can be discerned; but in any case, because the social setting may affect the information which he receives, the field worker is duty-bound to detail in his interview notes the exact social context in which it was conducted.

The collector should also be aware that the evasiveness of an informant or the incompleteness or inaccuracy of his information will usually vary inversely with the degree of rapport which has been established. At the beginning, when he has little trust in the collector, an informant may be diffident in revealing the extent of his knowledge on a specific subject and may deny practices and beliefs which he has reason to think may result in the collector's laughing at him; or he may boast or exaggerate in an attempt to raise his status in the eyes of the collector. In every case, and not only in the early stages, the collector's approach must be one of sympathy and respect. He must learn "to talk the language" (read: "appreciate the frame of reference") of his informants, and to converse with them on subjects and in terms familiar to them. In time the informants will relax their defenses; and, too, the collector will find that every interview session is in itself an occasion for improving rapport. The collector makes his informants feel important as collaborators, and well-conducted interviews serve as social occasions to which informants come to look forward.[9]

5. Ethnographic Dynamite

Certain subjects which comprise what anthropologists call "ethnographic dynamite" should be approached

9. B. A. Botkin, *Supplementary Instructions to The American Guide Manual for Folklore Studies* (n.p., 1938) p. 11.

cautiously and usually only after excellent rapport has been established. This "dynamite" will consist of "those phases of life which are the subject of deep emotional feelings or strong taboos"[10] and may include esoteric beliefs, secret rites, erotic matters (including obscene folklore) and matters which may be the cause of tension within a community, such as witchcraft, and devil lore. However interested the collector may be in these things (and frequently they involve areas of anxiety to the collector himself), he should avoid direct inquiry concerning them until he is on very familiar terms with his informants or until they proffer the information spontaneously. The content of "ethnographic dynamite" may vary greatly from one society to another, but the collector should be able to obtain sufficient cues from his informants during the early stages of his investigation to know which subjects are taboo. Though no guiding principles exist for helping him to avoid mistakes in this matter, a good general practice is for the collector to select in the early stages of his activities only those topics and situations which will be least likely to lead him into emotionally-laden subject matter.[11] In so doing he must be careful, however, not to give his informants the feeling that he lacks interest in these subjects. He should, indeed, indicate his interest by mentioning them occasionally, but to avoid doing so in a manner which makes it appear as if he is trying to draw the information out of them. They will recognize his curiosity and, when they feel secure in their relationship with him, they will want to satisfy it. If, however, he pretends to be ignorant of or uninterested in such matters, his informants may interpret this as meaning that he finds the subject matter distasteful, and out of respect for his feelings they may avoid those subjects.

10. Piddington, Vol. 2, p. 551.
11. Piddington, Vol. 2, p. 551.

6. Length of Interviews

Though usually the length of an interview is resolved by its participants, the collector may on occasion find himself wondering whether he has allowed a session to run on too long. There is no set of rules for determining the length of an interview.

The collector should take into account the informant's occupation, for if it involves his full attention it is obvious that he cannot be interviewed at the same time. For this reason women informants will usually comprise the majority of the collector's daytime interviewees. Most male informants (excepting unemployed, elderly, retired, and invalid persons) will usually have to be interviewed during after-work hours. In such cases, however, fatigue may become an important factor. Depth probing, for example, usually requires not only the full cooperation but also the full awareness and attentiveness of the informant. A tired informant is not the best interviewee; it may be necessary to restrict interviews with such persons to very short periods. In keeping such a consideration in mind, the collector need not necessarily keep his eye on the clock in the process; his sensitivity to signs of weariness on the part of the informant should be the cue to calling an interview session to an end. If, however, the informant is in the middle of describing some particularly complex situation, it is certainly better to finish the matter under discussion than stop in the middle and have to struggle at some future date to pick up the threads.

Sometimes the size of the interview project and the time which the collector has to remain in the field will be a prime consideration. If the collector is in the middle of recording a long personal history from an informant and has only a few weeks left to his stay in the field, he may be forced to conduct several long sessions a day. If, however, the collector's remaining time in the field is not a factor it is certainly better to restrict each interview to only a few hours a day at the most, and to conduct as many such sessions as seems necessary to obtain the data needed by the collector for his problem's solution. In every case, however, the major considerations in determining the length of interviews must be the informant's health, convenience, commitments, motivations, and degree of adjustment to the interview situation.

7. Notation of Interview Data

The notation of interview data may take several forms. Where informants are inhibited by note-taking, the collector will have to wait until each session is over before he can set down his notes on paper. Such sessions will, however, have to be relatively short because of memory retention problems, though with experience a rather great deal can be remembered without notes of any kind. Usually, however, once rapport has been established and the collector's role is clear to the informant, he will be permitted to take notes during the session itself. These may consist of extensive commentary (in which case some shorthand system will have to be employed) or simply of short phrases, key remarks in extenso, and mnemonic references of various kinds. Whether or not notes are made during the session itself, the major job of interview notation will have to take place after the session is over and preferably immediately thereafter. For further aids to the notation of interviews, see section 4 of the previous chapter.

The recording of interviews by sound equipment is certainly the best means. It permits the permanent recording of huge chunks of interview conversation and commentary exactly as stated and, should the collector miss anything mentioned during the interview, a playback of the recording will permit the omission to be corrected. It also enables the collector to study the natural use of folklore materials in the context of actual speech (e.g., proverbial expressions, jokes, tales, beliefs, etc.) as well as the differences between everyday and performance speech patterns. And, too, it presents the best if not the only way in which the collector may check on his own interviewing techniques. By objectively analyzing and evaluating the recorded interviews, he should be able to recognize the faults or weakness in his techniques and attempt to correct these in future interview sessions.

8. Noting the Circumstances of the Interview

Whether interview data is recorded by hand note-taking or by sound equipment, certain information should be noted concerning the circumstances of the interview situation. This information consists of identification data, and context data. The following list[12] may be used as a guide to the specific data to be noted:

1. Name, age, sex, occupation and address of interviewee (s).
2. Source of contact information.
3. Date and time of interview (as a practical matter each page of any notes taken should be dated).
4. Place where interview was conducted (if not at home of interviewee).
5. Description of social context covering all persons present at interview (see Chapter VI, section 5).
6. Description of physical context (see Chapter VI, section 5).

12. For a similar guide to interview notes, see Herbert Halpert and George Herzog, *Folksong Questionnaire* (n.p., 1939).

7. Comments on other circumstances of the interview, including techniques used by the collector, informant's general attitude, feelings and attitude of the collector.

In describing the circumstances of follow-up interviews with the same informant, the collector may omit all identification data except the interviewee's name.

9. Personal History Documents

One of the most important contributions which the field worker can make to folklore studies is the gathering of data for use in personal history documents. As they apply to the field of folklore, such documents may be defined as the story of the life (or some part of it) of an individual folklore informant. The data for these documents are obtained mainly by the use of interview methods, supplemented in varying degrees by observational techniques and library research. It is from such data that we can begin to appreciate the many factors which go into the making of a traditional performer and from which we shall some day learn, after enough such documents have been compiled, what it is that makes one performer a star among lessor figures in the community of tradition.

Personal history documents usually fall into one of the following three categories:

1. *LIFE HISTORIES*: Full-scale histories or thumbnail sketches of the lives of individual tradition bearers. Such works may be biographical, autobiographical, or a combination of both. Because of the great amount of work involved, few full-length works

have been compiled.[13] Because the informant who tells his life history will necesarily have forgotten much relevant material from his early life (the period during which the essential shaping of his life took place), the different periods of his history will be treated unevenly. During the past decade an increasing interest in such works by western folklorists has resulted in the publication of a fair number of thumb-nail sketches of varying size and scope.[14]

2. *EPISODIC WORKS*: Emphasis is placed on only one period of an informant's life, usually a key one. Few such works have been published, but they could contribute much to the study of the manner in which folklore materials function in the experiential frame of reference of the individual tradition bearer.[15] Examples of such studies which might be undertaken include a sailor's experiences during a voyage at sea, a cowboy's experiences on a cattle drive, or a convict's

13. The Lomaxes, John and Alan, have pioneered in this work with their biographical studies of Huddie Ledbetter and Jelly Roll Morton, and more recently Jean Ritchie has published a marvelous autobiographical study of her own family. Russian folklorists have examined the life and works of individual storytellers, and the results of their work has been summed up by M. K. Azadovsky, *Eine sibrische Märchenerzälerin* (Helsinki, 1926), F.F.C. No. 68.

14. See, for example, Richard M. Dorson's sketches of several of his informants in his various books and articles containing tales collected in Negro communities in Michigan and Arkansas; George Korson included vivid sketches of his main informants in *Minstrels of the Mine Patch* (Philadelphia, 1938; reprinted Hatboro, Pa., 1964) and *Coal Dust on the Fiddle* (Philadelphia, 1943). See also my article on "William Robbie: Folk Artist of the Buchan District, Aberdeenshire" in *Folklore in Action* (Philadelphia, 1962), pp. 101-111. Most recently excellent sketches of traditional folksingers have appeared in booklets of notes accompanying recordings of their folksongs.

15. The best of these, Frederick P. Harlow's *The Making of A Sailor* (Salem, 1928), is an autobiographical study of his years as a sailor. Similar autobiographical sketches of cowboys, lumberjacks, and other "occupational folk" are so numerous as to prevent documenting them here. But none of these is the work of a folklorist consciously attempting to produce an episodic work As such they are neither documented or analyzed from a folklorist's point of view.

informant in candid circumstances during actual performance, during interview sessions, at work, and in his Sunday
best; and where photographs of the informant exist prior
to his meeting with the collector, permission should be
obtained to have copies made for potential publication.

The biggest problem to the folklorist wishing to collect
data for a personal history document is selecting his "informant."[18] For full scale life histories or episodic works,
the collector will normally be drawn to the star performers
of a community. Since most folk communities rarely have
more than one such talent, the collector may have very
little choice. If a genuine choice exists, however, the
collector may base his decision on ability to verbalize,
attitude of cooperation, motivation, condition of health,
age, memory retention, personality, and accessiblity of the
informants. After carefully weighing all of these factors,
the collector will probably choose the individual whose
credentials offer the greatest promise of the successful
completion of a difficult project.

The collector should not overlook the average tradition
bearer as a potential figure for personal-history interviewing. Such people will supply the collector with a base for
comparing star performers to lesser figures in a community.
The basis for selecting average informants for personal-
history documentation includes all the criteria mentioned
above plus an analysis of how typical such persons are as
tradition bearers in the cultural matrix of the community.

In selecting informants for the recording of topical
studies, the collector must take into account whether or
not the situation or activity to be described is the domain
of specialists. If specialists are the only ones with such
information, then there is little point in working with
non-specialists. Where, however, the workings of a specific
activity or situation are known both to specialists and to a

18. Kluckhohn, "The Personal Document," p. 114 ff.

lesser degree to the community in general, the collector
would do well to select representatives of both groups for
his project.

Collectors with only short periods to spend in the field
will not have the time to do full scale-life histories or
episodic works; but they can be of great service in obtaining thumbnail sketches (of varying lengths) of the lives
of their informants. Indeed, the obtaining of such data
should become part of the field worker's standard procedure in collecting from his informants. To assist in
this work, the collector may use the following list as an
outline for the data to be garnered during personal history
interviews.[19]

1. Name and present address
2. Place and date of birth
3. Members of family
4. Family history
5. Ethnic ancestry
6. Education
7. Places of residence and travel
8. Occupational history
9. Awards and honors received
10. History of illnesses in family
11. Property and wealth achievements
12. Special skills and interests
13. Church membership and activity
14. Membership and activity in other organizations
15. Key points in life
16. Motivational aspirations and goals
17. Description of informant's status as a tradition
    bearer in the various communities in which he
    has lived

19. For a related list, oriented more in terms of the community in which
the informant lives, see Halpert and Herzog, *Folksong Questionnaire*
(n.p., 1939).

18. Sketch of informant's character
19. Description of informant (including photographs)
20. Folklore materials in informant's repertory.

While most of the above data can be obtained by direct questioning, it is better to get the informant talking freely about his life, thereby placing such data in a fuller context of subjective meaning. Points omitted by the informant can then be elicited by direct questions.

10. Collecting Folklore Materials

At the beginning of this chapter, it was stated that "though the interview situation may be an artificial one for observing performance, it is at the same time the only natural context for eliciting information from an informant." Part of that information which the collector-interviewer seeks is the materials of folklore. For this reason, collecting the materials themselves usually develops directly out of the normal interview situation.

This is not intended to be a contradiction of any statements made in the previous chapter which indicated that the natural performance context is best. Ideally, one would also like to be able to collect the materials in such contexts, but to attempt to do so may so affect the situation as to change it from a natural to an artificial context. This is especially true in the case of collecting the longer items of folklore—ballads and tales—when they are performed in natural semi-formal and informal contexts. For this reason, the collector must remain content with being able to collect only observation data in such contexts and reserve the collecting of folklore materials for the interview situation.

Many suggestions for collecting information in the interview context have already been given in this chapter, and insofar as folklore materials are considered part of that information, the advice will also apply to them. The rest of this chapter will supplement that advice with other suggestions for the collecting of the materials of folklore.

Audience Contexts

Various collectors have indicated that it is usually a good idea to have some kind of audience present while collecting folklore. The audience in such cases should be persons who would normally be present when the informant is performing in natural contexts. By their presence the collector's exoteric effect on the informant is minimized, thereby permitting the latter to perform in a more relaxed manner and atmosphere.

The performance of certain materials, especially "ethnographic dynamite," may be considerably inhibited by the presence of an audience in the interview situation. In a natural context for the performance of certain "dynamite" materials there will usually be a specific type of audience present, such as members of the same sex group in the performance of obscene materials, but an attempt to duplicate that audience for a collecting session may fail in its purpose. Some informants may prefer not to have it generally known, even to their friends and family, that they are supplying such materials to the collector. In such cases it is necessary for the collector to arrange a session at which only he and the informant will be present.

Non-Audience Context

There are, however, many informants who will not pass on certain materials or information pertaining to them even in the socially restricted context of the collector-informant situation. The inherent shyness of many country folk before strangers is only intensified in such contexts.

The collector is then faced with the problem of creating a non-interview, non-observation context, in which the informant performs or talks by himself to a non-audience. However impossible this may seem on first thought, such a context can be created. The collector makes his equipment available to the informant for him to record privately.[20] If the collector has at least two recording machines with him in the field, one can be lent to the informant for this purpose, or it can be left at the collector's residence with the informant given permission to drop in to use it whenever he so wishes. Or, in a collector-informant situation, should the informant balk at performing certain items with the collector present, the collector can simply absent himself and permit the informant to record without any audience. In my recording of children's rhymes and games from a group of twelve and thirteen year old girls, an impasse developed when the girls started whispering among themselves. Remembering my own experiences as a child, together with the knowledge of my own children's secretiveness when it comes to certain materials in their repertories, I realized that the girls were whispering rhymes which they considered obscene or which they felt they could not recite in my presence. I informed them that I knew what they were whispering about and, though I could appreciate their reluctance to perform such pieces in my presence, that such materials were as important to my collecting project as were the more innocent materials. I suggested that they record the materials by themselves after I left the room, and that I wouldn't return until they called for me. My proposal was accepted. I left the tape recorder running and showed

20. I have used this technique many times in my field work, and Roger Abrahams utilized it effectively for collecting Negro folklore in South Philadelphia (see his unpublished dissertation *Negro Folklore from South Philadelphia, A Collection and Analysis* [University of Pennsylvania, 1962], Chapter I.)

the girls where to stand when they performed their pieces into the microphone. Almost an hour passed before I was called back into the room, during which time they had filled a reel of tape with their own peer-group erotica and esoterica.

In some cases an informant may be willing to recite certain "ethnographic dynamite" materials for the collector, but will not permit a permanent sound record (as with a tape recorder or other equipment) to be made of his performance. The collector should never badger an informant to do something which he is dead set against doing. Instead, the field worker must use other means for collecting such items. He can take down the text (and tune, if the piece is a song) in writing or shorthand or, lacking ability to notate music (a factor which is all too common even among folksong and folkmusic specialists), he can ask the informant to allow him to use the sound equipment to record only the melody. The informant can then whistle or hum the tune, or play it on any instrument which he can handle and which happens to be at hand. In one case, when even this ruse did not work, I later asked one of my informant's daughters, who knew all the tunes to her mother's songs, to permit me to record her rendition of those tunes. More gregarious and less inhibited than her mother, the daughter complied by humming the tunes into the microphone of my tape recorder. Though I would have preferred to obtain both texts and tunes from the same informant, the separate recording of them from two related persons was better than just the texts alone.

Performance by the Collector

Many collectors establish a more natural context for collecting by exchanging stories and songs with their informants. Informants are just as pleased to hear items unknown to them as they are likely to be proud of the fact that they can perform pieces which the collector has not previously heard. Indeed, such performance on the part of the collector can serve purposes other than social camaraderie. Items performed by the collector can serve as leads to the possible performance of versions of those same items by the informant; or such performance can be used in a field experiment to see which items are picked up by informants and pass into their repertories, and what changes they undergo in the process. To one of my informants I sang several verses of a fishing song which I had collected in fragmentary form a few weeks earlier. In adding the song to my own repertory I had expanded on the fragmentary text. A month later I collected the same song, including my interpolations, from another woman at the other end of town. In checking the matter, I found that the first informant had learned the song from me in that one hearing and had passed it on to the second informant. Obviously, the lesson to be learned from such an experience is that whenever a collector performs for his informants he would be well advised to make a note of that fact, including information as to the names of pieces and the versions which he performed. Then, should his informants add any of those pieces to their own repertories, the items can be traced and documented by himself or other collectors following him.

The collector who performs for his informants, whether by his own choice or at their request, should attempt to keep such performance to a minimum. The field worker's job is to collect the materials and data of folklore from his informants, not to assist them to collect from him. The development of rapport and social camaraderie may call for the collector performing, but it should never interfere with his field objectives. The performing talents of a collector may be an asset in his work with informants (see Chapter IV); but it must never be allowed to handicap that work.

Exact Recording of Materials

The anecdote related above raises a point which is now so taken for granted in professional folklore circles that it is rarely mentioned. But insofar as this *Guide* may be used by non-academic folklorists it is a point which cannot be repeated too often. The field worker is bound to record everything he collects in the exact form given to him by an informant. His notes must be an exact transcription of their performance. For the scientific purposes of folklore he is allowed no leeway on this point. There is only one way to transcribe materials: exactly as heard. Should a collector wish to add some of his collectanea to his own repertory (a non-folkloristic objective), he may do so in any manner he wishes, but the two roles—folklorist and performer—should be kept entirely separate.

While the accurate and scientific recording of longer folklore items is usually taken for granted, this advice must also be extended to the shorter, non-performance items. Too often, for example, collections are published in which superstitions or riddles are not reported in the exact words of informants. Instead, they are generalized to what the collector believes is the proper form for the item. The following hypothetical situation can serve to illustrate my point. A collector walking down a street with one of his informants is suddenly cautioned: "If that cat crosses your path, you're in for bad luck." The collector notices that the cat referred to is a black one, and writes on his note pad: "It's bad luck if a black cat crosses one's path." The inaccuracies of such notation are fraught with danger. It may well be that the crossing of one's path by any color of cat is considered bad luck by the informant, or it may refer only to cats crossing from left to right in front of a person, or it may be that only black cats crossing from left to right are interpreted as bad luck by the informant. There are in fact four possibilities for the form which this superstition may take.[21] By his having generalized the form to only one of these possibilities, the collector may be incorrect. The correct procedure to follow in such a case is to take down the superstition in the informant's own words, note the exact situation in which it occurred (as far as that is possible), and then check with the informant at that time or later in order to ascertain the exact content of that belief in his own frame of reference. The collector can then correct his original notation (again, preferably in the informant's own words). When such a superstition is published, the collector can indicate that all remarks in quotations are cited exactly as obtained from the informant; when the informant's statement of a belief is not in an understandable form outside the context of a full conversation, then the collector can rephrase the informant's words into a more generalized form, but should indicate that he has done so.[22]

Selective vs. "Vacuum Cleaner" Collecting

A question which comes up frequently in conversations and discussions about collecting is: "What materials should the field worker collect from his informants?" In many areas, modern materials spread by commercial communications media have infused the traditional repertories of folk performers. Should the collector act as a "vacuum cleaner" and collect everything which his informants know or wish to perform for him, or should he be selective

21. For a sampling of the wide range of superstitions relative to cats crossing one's path, see *The Frank C. Brown Collection of North Carolina Folklore*, Vol. VI, ed. Wayland D. Hand (Durham, 1961), nos. 3808-3845, (pp. 507-512).

22. I have gone into the matter of collecting superstitions in greater detail in the article "The Collecting of Superstitious Beliefs," *Keystone Folklore Quarterly* IX (No. 1, Spring, 1964), pp. 13-22.

and collect only those pieces which he believes or knows to be traditional? Several factors bear upon this question: the collector's specific problem, the amount of time he has to spend in the field, the type of collecting project (survey or depth) , and the collector's training and experience.

If a collector's problem is to study the changes which have taken place in the oral traditions of the peoples of a certain region, group, or community, he should document and collect everything in the oral repertory of his informants. If, however, his problem is to discover what remains of past traditions in the memories of the people being investigated, he will attempt to collect only the older traditions and avoid anything which he believes not to be part of those traditions. If his collecting project calls for only a short stay in the field or involves making a broad survey of the materials being circulated by his potential informants, the collector may not have the time to collect everything his informants know, and he may therefore decide that he will record only the materials which he feels fit his definition of "traditional."

It is on this last point—the question of definition—that the whole matter comes to a head. If the collector's definition is a very narrow one in which he has placed strict limitations as to the age of materials, the degree to which they have circulated and the amounts and kinds of changes which have been made in them, then, depending upon his experience and knowledge in passing such judgments, he may be able to exclude from his collectanea a portion of the materials offered to him by his informants. But such judgments include subjective inferences and interpretations. As has been stressed before, the ideal for the field worker—as a field worker—is objectivity, not subjectivity; facts, not inferences and interpretation. They may follow in his analysis of the materials after he has left the field, but that is part of another and later step in problem-solving and need not be his concern in the data-collecting stage.

Even if one forgets the admonition against subjectivity in the data collecting stage, no matter how knowledgeable and experienced the collector is there are likely to be holes in his ability to make certain judgments. It will be necessary for a collector to have near-total familiarity with collectanea before he can say that such and such an item is non-traditional simply because there is no record of its prior existence in tradition. Even if he does have such knowledge of previous collectanea, he has no certainty that a piece is not traditional just because it has never before been collected. Every experienced collector knows that even after hundreds of years of field work, there are still many traditional items in existence which have never fallen into a collector's net. Indeed, every field trip turns up a few such items, and there is no reason to believe that we are anywhere near the bottom of the barrel. In passing judgment as to pieces not previously reported, the collector can of course call on his knowledge of form, content, style, and structure in determining whether or not an item is traditional. But even here he may find that he can be fooled—that on rare occasions non-traditional pieces have been so artfully created in the idiom of tradition that it would be impossible to recognize such items without specific knowledge of their non-traditional origin.

The collector might then argue that he can at least disregard those items which are modern popular pieces; but he can be certain of the modernity of only those items which he has read or heard and which he can trace to some popular source. Even in his own cultural subgroup there are likely to be in circulation thousands of modern popular items of which he has no knowledge. Before he

can expect to make such judgments in cultures other than
his own, he will have to spend much time reading and
listening to everything modern and circulated via mass
communication media, time which very few collectors
ever have in the field. And even if his definition is broad
enough to recognize that modern popular pieces occasionally do pass into a widespread oral tradition, he will
be unable to determine whether or not certain modern
pieces have in fact passed into tradition and undergone
the changes implicit in the process until he has collected
those items and compared them with the standardized,
commercial, mass communication forms of the originals.

The collector with limited time to spend in the field
may still prefer to make such judgments (as we all do on
occasion), even after admitting the imperfection of his
knowledge and experience in inferentially and subjectively
making decisions of this order; but in so doing he should
not delude himself that he has collected everything
which his definition permits. The only way to do
that would be to apply the "vacuum cleaner" approach and
collect everything offered to him. Then, if he has erred, at
least it will have been in the direction of "too much"
rather than "too little" and the matter can be corrected
by a weeding-out process later on. If he has erred in the
direction of "too little," the situation may be nearly
irrevocable and even return trips may not enable him to
collect the materials which he omitted on his first trip.

There are also several other good reasons for applying
the "vacuum cleaner" approach to collecting. In attempting to make selections in the field, the collector will be
forced to stop his informants at times and inform them that
"That isn't quite what I'm looking for." In doing so he
will not only disturb the natural social and psychological
factors involved in his informants' ordering of the materials
in their repertories, but he may also unwittingly hurt his
informants' pride, or confuse them, neither of which will

help in maintaining rapport with them. And in explaining or defining the kinds of materials for which he is looking, he must contend with the imperfect comprehension which results from his informants' having neither his own training or knowledge which enables him to make the necessary discriminations. Such imperfect comprehension may result in his not being offered certain materials in which he would be interested, but which his informants have excluded from his consideration because they misunderstood his frame of reference.

If the collector is using modern sound equipment for recording his informants' materials, it is less time-consuming simply to record everything which they proffer rather than to hear each piece first before making a decision as to whether or not it should be recorded. A decision to do so will mean that the informant will have to repeat the item "for the record," during which time he might have been performing other pieces from his repertory.[23]

But perhaps the most important reason why a field worker should apply a "vacuum cleaner" in his collecting activities is that from such comprehensiveness it may be possible at a later date to determine inferentially certain factors involved in an informant's aesthetic. If one accepts that fact that tradition bearers have an aesthetic, then an examination of the pieces which they perform may supply

23. Before the day of modern mechanical sound recording devices it was probably impractical to take down everything recited or sung by informants. To do so would have been exceedingly time and energy consuming. In such cases, Y. L. Cahan suggested that the collector should listen to each item thoroughly before recording it, taking notes as the materials are recited for the first time. By such means the collector would know what to ask for when he actually took down the specific items, and could then avoid asking for those items in which he was not interested. This saved the collector the sometimes unpleasant task of rejecting materials directly and thereby enabled him to avoid the risk of offending an informant. (See Richard Bauman, "Y. L. Cahan's Instructions on the Collecting of Folklore," *NYFQ* (1962), pp. 287-288.) Cahan's comments still apply for those situations and occasions when a collector is unable to use mechanical recording devices.

clues necessary for solving that problem. If, for example, an informant indicates equal preference for older traditional pieces and modern songs in his repertory then it may be possible by intensive examination of those pieces to determine what they have in common that endeared them to the informant. We will then be one step closer to understanding the aesthetic of that informant. But such inferential determination of his aesthetic will be possible only if a record is made of all materials in his repertory and not only those which the folklorist believes to be traditional.

In collecting folklore materials it is preferable for the field worker to permit the informant to determine his own natural order for performing the items in his repertory. By so doing it may be possible to decipher the manner in which he orders his materials and discover what factors contribute to it. While it may not always be possible to allow the informant the full freedom of ordering his own materials, even sessions in which the collector is seeking to obtain specific items should be flexible enough to permit the informant to perform additional pieces as they come to mind.

In order to study the range of variation in the performance of a song or tale by a single informant, the collector is advised to have selected items in an informant's repertory repeated in various contexts and over a period of time. Ideally, it would be preferable if the collector could get an informant to do so for every item in his repertory; this however may be possible only in the case of informants with relatively small repertories.

11. Case History of Folklore Materials

As has been indicated earlier in this chapter, the field worker should be interested not only in the materials of folklore, but also in as much relevant information as he can obtain about those materials. While the purpose of this work is not to supply a questionnaire for obtaining that information, there are certain important data which a collector should try to obtain when possible. This information may be considered the "case history" of the materials. Since the context in which this information will be obtained is that of an interview session, obviously the first data to be noted should be the circumstances of the interview. And at some time in his association with the informant the collector should also obtain at least a thumbnail sketch of the informant's life history. The case history for the individual items in the informant's repertory may include the following data:[24]

1. What is the informant's title or name for the item? Does he know any other names for the same piece? How does he refer to it if he has no name for the item?

2. Does the informant classify the item by kind? What are the informant's genre groupings (his terms and definitions)?

3. Is the item merely "remembered," or is it still functioning or being performed in a vital tradition? If it is still being performed, when, where, how often and in what contexts? Has the informant ever performed that item on radio, television, on a stage or in a formal public situation?

4. How, when, where and from whom was it learned? Did the informant hear it more than once from the same person or from different persons before first performing it himself? Did the informant write down the text (or tune) as an aid to learning it?

24. This listing has been adapted, for the most part, from Halpert and Herzog's *Folksong Questionnaire*.

(If so, the collector should try to obtain the original written form or get permission to copy it). Was it learned from a mass communication media source?

5. What does the item mean to the informant? If descriptive or narrative, does it refer to an actual place or happening? Does the informant believe it to be true? Why?

6. Does the informant know more than one form for the item? Does he know variant texts (or tunes)? In the case of a song or ballad, does he perform the same text to different tunes?

7. What is the informant's aesthetic evaluation of the piece? Why does he like it? Why does he perform it? What emotion does it evoke in the informant?

8. Did the informant make any conscious changes in the item since he first heard it? Why, when, how? Has he combined parts of different texts (or tunes), or has he added several items together to make a longer piece?

Obviously not all of the above questions can be asked for all genres of folklore. And, too, it will be up to the collector to determine the exact wording of the questions necessary to obtain the information. But no matter how skillful the collector is in wording the questions, he should not expect to obtain answers to all of them. Responses will vary from informant to informant, from question to question, and from item to item; the more intelligent and sensitive informants will probably give more and fuller answers. But even short, relatively incoherent, or rambling answers may supply some useful data towards the solution of a folkloristic problem.

The main problem relative to obtaining a case history of a folklore item or items is determining when to ask the questions. Should they be asked at the session in which the items are performed, and if so, should it be immediately after each piece is performed or should they be delayed until the informant has finished performing all of his materials for that session? To interrupt the normal flow of materials by questioning after each item is performed is to lose an opportunity to study the informant's manner of ordering his materials; and it may also inhibit further performance at that session. Logically it would seem, questions should be saved until the end of the session. If many items have been collected during the session, it may take longer for the questioning session than for the performing session. In such a case it may be necessary to carry the questioning over to another day.

On the other hand, the best moment to obtain information from an informant about his view of the content of a folklore item may be immediately after he has performed it or listened to a playback of a recording of that performance. At that moment the latent content is near the surface and it may be obtained easily by encouraging the informant to talk and freely associate.

The decision as to when to obtain case histories for individual items in an informant's repertory will have to be made in terms of the specific problems which the collector has set for himself in the field. Perhaps the best solution is to conduct some sessions with case histories obtained after each piece is performed, and other sessions with questioning reserved until the performance part of the sessions has ended. The collector can then take his cue as to which method is better for any one informant from the reactions of that informant.

Even if the field worker desires to ask all relevant questions for every item he collects, the time he has to spend in the field or with any single informant may be limited, in which case he will have to make a choice between collecting more materials and fewer case histories of those items, or fewer materials and fuller case histories. He will probably compromise and only bother to get full case histories for those items which most interest him personally, or from the informants who seem most able to answer the questions fully.

12. Transcribing Recorded Interviews to Paper

While the collector may have to take down folklore materials by hand in many contexts, during the interview context he should be able to record the materials with the use of sound equipment. When doing so, however, he should transcribe the collected materials to paper as soon as possible, and preferably the same day. This immediate transcription will serve several purposes. The informant's pronunciation and dialect may be such that the collector will have problems in transcribing texts from the tape recorder, though he may have had little or no trouble with understanding his informant during the session. The greater the time delay between the session and the transcription, the greater the loss of memory relating to what was said or performed. The collector who does immediate transcriptions has the advantage of his memory to assist him with deciphering dialect or pronunciation; and even when the collector has neither of these problems, there will usually be obscure words or localisms which can be explained only by the informant or some other native of the community. The collector can read his transcription of the text to the informant from whom it was collected, ascertain that he has taken it down correctly, and obtain explanations or definitions for any obscure or local terms. If the collector puts off doing this for any length of time, he may find that additional materials have piled-up so quickly that to catch up with transcribing might mean taking several days off from his field work. However, this problem is pretty well taken care of if the collector develops the habit of making each day's transcriptions before retiring for the evening.

13. Safety Copies of Notes and Recordings

The collector should provide himself with safety copies of all recordings and notes made in the field. In the case of handwritten notes and transcriptions, this can be achieved by making carbon copies, ditto masters, or using multiple reproduction sets when data or materials are being written or typed out. In the case of tape recordings, a second machine will come in handy in making copies of original tapes and, even if the copies are not quite as good as the originals, an inferior copy is better than none at all should the originals get lost or be accidentally erased. All safety copies of materials and data, whether handwritten, typed, or recorded, should be sent to an archive or to the collector's home so that should he lose his records while in the field or on the return trip home copies will still be available for him to work with.

CHAPTER VIII

Supplementary Field Methods

In the course of the preceding chapters, the major field methods and techniques available to the folklorist have been discussed in some detail. In addition to these, there exist several supplementary techniques for obtaining leads to informants and for collecting materials and data.

1. Mass Communications Media

Though mass communications media are often decried by folklorists as the bane of an oral tradition, the collector is in a position to make constructive use of them to further his own work. Because he is a visitor interested in what most people would consider esoterica or exotica, and because he is supposed to be an academic authority, he makes good copy for newspapers, magazines, radio, and television. On the rare occasions when he may have to make the first contact, the collector is advised to trace down the various news media during the early days after his arrival in a community.

The collector's interest in these communications media does not lie in the ego satisfaction that he may derive from their spreading his name, like that of a visiting dignitary, throughout the land. Their value to him lies in their ability to assist in bringing his work to the attention of the population, to spread word of his mission, to ease his acceptance in the community and, through a combination of all of these, to assist potential informants to make themselves known to the collector. A review of these media will be given below in order to indicate the specific manner in which they have been used in the past and may continue to be used by collectors in the course of their field work.

Newspapers and Magazines

Practically every small community in the literate world either has one or more of its own daily, weekly, bi-weekly, or monthly newspapers or magazines, or has distributed within its boundaries one or more such publications from a larger nearby community or a national publishing house. As a stranger from another region or country, the collector is an excellent source of news copy. Reporters assigned to the collector will report his arrival, his place of origin, the purpose of his visit to the community, his status in his discipline, the expected length of his stay, his opinion of the community in which he is working, and other miscellaneous information which may be of interest to the readers of those publications. I was in the Buchan District of northeastern Scotland less than two days when reporters from three different local and regional newspapers descended on my new-found residence to interview me and my family. I took advantage of these interviews to explain my reasons for coming to that part of Scotland, to establish my role as a collector of "old-fashioned" songs and stories, and to indicate my affiliation with the School of Scottish Studies as the national cultural body overseeing my activities. In the first interview (fairly certain that there would be many more to come), I did not make any direct appeals for help or for leads to informants. Despite this, and as a result of the printed interviews which appeared a few days later, I received seven letters and ten phone calls from persons who either wanted to perform for me or who were related to persons whom they wanted me to hear. Two weeks later, the same reporters visited again. This time I took advantage of their interviews to make a directed appeal for songs, stories, and leads to informants. Almost immediately I received over thirty letters and phone calls, which eventually led me to a wide range of materials and several excellent informants.

After the field worker has been in a community long enough to have collected a variety of material, he can ask the newspapers to cooperate with his collecting project by publishing stories about his field work activities. Here the collector can talk about some of his informants (after first obtaining permission to use their names) and the kinds of materials he has obtained from them, and perhaps convince the reporter to include examples of their stories and songs. When possible, the collector should refer to informants who were located as the result of having seen the earlier articles on his work. This will serve to encourage other potential informants to come forward.

The collector may also use these newspaper interviews to make appeals for specific kinds of materials and even for published books and printed materials which may assist him with his work By this means I was able to locate one of Gavin Greig's relatives who had a set of the extremely scarce volumes, *Folk-Song of the North-East*,[1]

1. Gavin Greig, *Folk Song of the North-East*, 2 vols. (Peterhead, 1909, 1914). Only 42 sets of these volumes were published. As a result of obtaining these volumes, I received the permission of the original publishers and Greig's heirs and have republished the 2 volumes in one (Folklore Associates, Hatboro, Penna., 1963).

which I very badly needed as a base for making a comparison between the materials which I collected with those found fifty years earlier in the same region.

The travelling collector, or a collector able to spend only a few months in a community, cannot be as leisurely in his approach. Usually the first interview will have to serve both to establish his role in the community and to make appeals for materials and informants.

But whether the collector's stay is long or short or whether he is attempting to reach only a small part or the whole of the local population, he will generally be overwhelmed by the size of the response to these published interviews. And he must be prepared to answer every response to his request for materials or informants. Should the number be great, he may select the most promising leads to follow up with personal visits, and answer the others by telephone or letters. To be delinquent in doing so may well result in the discourtesy of the collector strongly affecting his attempts to establish rapport in the community.

As in the case of newspapers in our own country, the collector can expect to find that many newspapers are interested in obtaining bizarre stories. Though the collector may be interested in obtaining leads to witchcraft and devil beliefs, he must be warned against giving the newspapers an opportunity to ruin his entire project by sensationalizing such interests. He will also find that rarely will he be quoted exactly; reporters frequently will put words into his mouth and quote him as saying things which may strongly negate any good will which he built.

The collector should stick to safe subjects when he is being interviewed, referring only to folksongs, simple tales, children's rhymes, riddles, and the like. When the collector refers to any of his informants or to the community in which he is working, he must do so with respect and sincerity, never condescendingly or with ridicule. Reporters who attempt to sensationalize the work of the collector should be discouraged from returning for later interviews. Since, however, the collector is likely to be good copy for the full length of his stay in a community, he will find that certain reporters usually will be willing to cooperate fully with him, to check stories before they are published, and to follow his suggestions as to how the stories should be written.

An even better method of promoting his work is for the collector to write his own articles or columns for publication in the pages of the local papers. Resident collectors have been able to use this means effectively for contacting informants throughout the area reached by their articles.[2] By writing his own articles, the collector will be certain of their content and can then blame any mistaken impressions only on his own errors. It will, furthermore, give the collector an opportunity to publish as much collectanea as he feels is necessary to maintain and create interest in his work, as well as permit him to publicize his informants, which may serve as an aid to establishing and maintaining good will and rapport. Some informants, however, may be rather timid about such publicity, and the collector is advised to obtain their permission before publishing their names or materials.

The collector should make a point of systematically reading all papers and magazines in his area. Many small "country" newspapers are actually folk newspapers publishing local songs, poetry, stories, and reports of local folklore events, all of which will help to keep the collector

2. For example, Gavin Greig wrote weekly articles on folksongs in the pages of the *Buchan Observer* between 1907 and 1911, publishing songs sent in by readers whom he later visited to record their singing of the same songs. In America, Vance Randolph, Ray Wood, Gordon Wilson, Allan Trout, and others have effectively used the newspaper columns to collect folklore and obtain leads to informants.

informed of certain levels of folklore transmission in his area, as well as supplying him with leads to events which he may wish to observe.

Radio and Television

Radio and television also present the collector with a news outlet to assist in publicizing his role and reaching potential informants.[3] Where the collector can arrange to be interviewed in person for a radio or television program, he will be able to control the content at least so far as his own comments are concerned. An interesting interview, in addition to permitting a collector to reach even illiterate members of a fairly large audience, may also lead to other programs on which the collector can play tapes of his informants or perhaps have them appear in live performances. Also, a collector with imagination and some knowledge of programming techniques may be able to sell a radio or television station on the idea of a documentary type of program in which the collector is able to perform a cultural service, show his informants to good advantage, and develop an interest in his field work in communities reached by the program.

There are several dangers in the use of these media. Most persons watching television and listening to radio have an inflated idea of the financial rewards made for those who appear on programs. Most small stations have no budget for news, cultural, or documentary programming, and only rarely will the collector be offered pay for appearing as a guest on such programs. Potential informants among listeners and viewers have no way of knowing this, and may feel that the collector is "making good

3. Alan Lomax found several of his finest folksong informants as the result of radio broadcasts, and Lowell Thomas made a very valuable collection of tall tales as a result of news broadcasts on which he told some of the stories received by him (these were published in *Tall Stories*, New York, 1945).

money" for such appearances; they will therefore expect payment for cooperating with the collector when they might otherwise have been willing to perform without payment. For this reason the collector is advised to avoid taking a prominent part in these programs and should let his informants play the star roles. Should the collector be a performer himself, it is better if he does not use these programs to perform the materials he has collected. A performance by the collector will make it appear as if his field work has been for the purpose of building his own repertory from which he will make money without recompensing his informants.

The intelligent collector should keep these points in mind when planning to use these media as a means of reaching potential informants; the positive effects of such programs will usually greatly outweigh any potentially negative effects on his collecting project.

2. Collecting from Children

Field workers in folklore who are not specialists in children's lore rarely take full advantage of their opportunities to collect from children. Yet among children there exists one of the most creative, continuous, and vital traditions in the entire field of folklore. For their own peer-group materials they are both the best and the only active source. Too often collectors take a short cut to collecting children's lore by obtaining it from adult informants. However, while such materials are valuable historically, adults are only inactive bearers of a remembered tradition, and the living tradition can be obtained only from children.

Because children's materials are so in-group oriented, there is a real challenge to the collector to obtain anything more than simply those materials which the children are willing to permit him to hear and observe. But children have a whole world of private beliefs, rhymes, and erotica which only a few sensitive and understanding adults are ever allowed to penetrate. By using his own children as an indirect entrée into the children's realm, by calling on his wife or a female assistant to take full advantage of the quasi "mother-child" relationship potential, and by employing the special techniques of the "induced context" and "non-audience" situation, the collector can add greatly to his own potentially limited access to the world of children's lore and fantasy.

Nor is this the limit to which children can be of value to the field worker. In addition to their roles as active bearers of their own peer-group esoterica, they are also inactive bearers of sometimes considerable amounts of adult folklore. Though they are obviously not the best bearers of such traditions (for stories and songs the collector is better advised to go to the adults themselves), the field worker can use them to conduct interesting field experiments tracing the transmission of certain materials from adults to children and then on to other children. But perhaps their most valuable potential contribution to the folklorist in terms of adult folklore is as contacts for supplying leads to the adult tradition-bearers involved in their lives. Sometimes such potential informants might never be brought into contact with the collector by any other means; and one of the first rules of the field worker is that he must be open at all times to any means by which he can increase his network of informants.

Highly organized and large-scale collecting projects involving thousands of school children have been successfully employed by folklore institutions in various parts of Europe.[4] Considerable children's and adult folklore,

4. Seán Ó Súilleabháin describes collecting from school children in Ireland, and Walter Anderson from school children in Estonia, in *Four Symposia on Folklore*, ed. Stith Thompson (Bloomington, 1953), pp. 10-12, 58-60.

as well as leads to superior adult informants, have been garnered in this manner. While such large-scale projects are not to be expected from the individual field worker, numerous cues may be taken from such work and applied to the smaller situation existing in almost any community in which there is a grade school. An attempt to obtain by other means the materials and information made available by the use of the technique described below might otherwise involve the full-time activities of the field worker.

The collector first approaches the headmaster or principal of the local grade school with the idea of conducting a folklore collecting program or competition among the students in his school. The children are to write down their own lore and collect adult lore from members of their family or neighbors. The schoolmaster should be given a clearly outlined plan of the entire project in which details are given for the kinds of materials in which the collector is interested as well as an indication of the supplementary information to be obtained for each of the items reported by the children (including the name, age, and address of each child and when, where, and from whom each item was collected). All other matters should be left to the discretion of the headmaster, with the collector acting only as an adviser. He should offer his services in training the teachers to conduct the instructional period in which the children are given the assignment, or ask if he may instruct the children himself. The headmaster may reject both of these training methods and suggest that the collector prepare an instructional booklet of which copies can be typed and given to each of the teachers at the school.

The matter of grading or judging the completed reports of the children should also be left to the discretion of the school authority; most teachers will be less interested in the quality or quantity of the materials turned in, and will emphasize neatness, penmanship, form of the report, and the amount of obvious interest or labor applied to the project by the students. In any case, the collector's real interest is in the reports themselves. He should try to obtain the original reports, or, failing that, ask to copy out of them any materials or information pertinent to his own work. By an inspection of the reports, the collector should be able to select those children who will probably prove to be the most cooperative and best sources for personal interviewing and collecting, and also determine which adult tradition bearers mentioned by the children are likely to become valuable informants.

In applying this method to my own field work in northeastern Scotland, I obtained 142 booklets of collectanea from local school children ranging in age from nine to fourteen. There was, of course, a fair amount of duplicated materials in many of the reports, indicating a widespread copying of materials from child to child as well as from standard printed sources. However, eleven of these reports contained excellent collections of primary source materials from which I was able to obtain a fine sampling of the rhymes, games, riddles, tongue twisters, taunts, and other lore in the repertories of that community's school children. From these eleven children I was later able to collect additional materials (including erotica) by applying the "induced context" and "non-audience" techniques described previously. And these reports also led me to interview twenty-three adult members of the community, five of whom turned out to be excellent informants with a wide range of song and tale traditions.

The method is not foolproof in turning up the best of the child tradition bearers. Many potentially fine child informants will be among those who are the most slovenly, lazy, or uninterested students. Their reports will in no way reflect their status as star tradition bearers among the children of the community. In addition, the reports of adult materials by the children will be uneven in quality. Where children have carefully taken down the exact words of their parents and relatives, the reports will be useful; more often, however, such reports will consist of useless half-remembered, half-gibberish phrases. But these disadvantages will be more than outweighed by the positive time- and energy-saving results in locating good informants among both children and adults in the community.

3. Questionnaires

Questionnaires have been used to collect folklore information since at least the first-half of the seventeenth century in Sweden, and in Germany since the nineteenth century.[5] At the present time they are used extensively by various European archives and folk museums.[6] Most of these questionnaires are concerned with some special subject or event about which highly specific information is wanted. The questionnaires are sent out to regular correspondents, both folk and non-folk. The latter group usually includes school teachers, priests, and students who administer the questionnaires in interviewing folk residents of their community, while the former group— farmers, laborers, and lumbermen—are themselves informants who supply the information from their own experiences and knowledge as well as soliciting information from other folk like themselves.[7]

5. E. J. Lindgren, "The Collection and Analysis of Folk-Lore," *The Study of Society: Methods and Problems* (London, 1939), p. 373.

6. *Four Symposia*, p. 10 (use of questionnaires in Ireland), p. 17 (use of questionnaires in Sweden).

7. *Four Symposia*, p. 17.

The main value of the highly organized use of these questionnnaires is their ability to obtain information in depth from a distance on almost every conceivable folklore subject, without having to send out trained field workers to conduct personal interviews. They must therefore be viewed as an expedient meant to obtain information when and where field workers cannot continually be active and present to obtain the same data. As such, they can appropriately be considered as auxiliaries to comprehensive field work by individual collectors.[8] This does not mean that they cannot be useful to the trained field worker. Where they are available from some organization in the country in which a collector is working, he should obtain those questionnnaires that apply to his own areas of interest. Because they are frequently detailed and based on a body of knowledge, they can serve to assist the collector in directing him to the kinds of information which may be obtained in the course of his own interviewing of informants. Their disadvantage is their fixed form and order of questions; the collector who uses them as a basis for his own interviews with informants adds the additional factor of flexibility, permitting him to follow up points raised by the informant which are not included in a questionnnaire, and changing both the order and content of questions when the circumstances call for that. Only trained respondents can begin to answer questionnaires with anything near the completeness of information which a collector can elicit by interview techniques. Rarely will the collector have the time to train or supervise his informants in their use. And the collector's presence makes it unnecessary to use them in the formal context for which they were designed.

In countries in which prepared questionnaires are not available the collector can prepare his own, or he can avail

8. E. J. Lindgren, p. 374, quoting from S. Erixon.

himself of the generalized questionnaires in various folklore and anthropological handbooks.[9]

4. Finding Lists

Closely related to the questionnaire, but far more widely used by collectors, are "finding lists." These usually consist of typical titles, opening lines, choruses, key phrases, or plot sketches which are recited to an informant as an aid to refreshing his memory. They are meant to suggest specific items which he can then perform in the variant or version known to him. In some cases the "finders" may suggest pieces to him other than those with which they are usually associated. The collector should, of course, welcome any item performed or recited in response to these "finders." And since there is no one correct version, the collector should make it clear to the informant that his version is as good as, or even better than, the one known to the collector.

To date too few finding lists have been published,[10] and collectors who compile their owns lists would be performing a service to their colleagues in the field by publishing them. No finding list can be complete, since there are numerous materials which have never been collected; but the fact that such lists can be only partial should not

---

9. G. P. Murdock et al, *Outline of Cultural Materials* (New Haven, 1950); *Notes and Queries on Anthropology*, Sixth Edition (London, 1951); Seán Ó Súilleabháin, *A Handbook of Irish Folklore* (Reprint edition, Hatboro, Pa., 1963); G. L. Gomme, *The Handbook of Folklore* (London, 1890).

10. See, for example, Fletcher Collins, Jr., "An Aid to the Discovery of Folk Song: A List of Finders for Traditional Ballads, Songs and Play-Parties in the Southeast," *SFQ* V (1941), pp. 235-250; Altha Lea McLendon, "A Finding List of Play-Party Games," *SFQ* VIII (1944), pp. 201-234; Richard Chase, "Amateur Collector's Guide," Chapter 6 in *American Folk Tales and Songs* (New York, 1956), pp. 228-235.

deter the collector from presenting them to other members of his discipline. In any case, they are usually designed merely to inspire an informant.

In drawing up finding lists of his own, a collector will often use as a base collections of materials previously compiled in that or nearby areas. Or, if no field work has previously been done in that area, he may draw on national collections, collections from culturally or linguistically related areas, or in some cases, from international indexes.

From discussions with a large number of collectors, I have found that most of them use such lists at the beginning of their field work in an area, or in their first contact with an informant. From my own experience, however, I have found finding lists even more useful as a means for drawing out an informant when his repertory appears to have been exhausted, or immediately before I am about to leave an area and can no longer use other and slower methods for eliciting those materials in an informant's repertory which are less commonly performed by him and therefore not available for immediate recall. During the first nine months of my stay in northeastern Scotland, I collected as much material from my main informants as my time, experience, and methods permitted me. During the last month, I began to use finding lists to elicit whatever materials may have been missed or forgotten. For a finding list of ballads and songs I used Gavin Greig's *Folk-Song of the North-East* and *Last Leaves*[11] as a base; for tales, the Aarne-Thompson Tale Type index;[12] for riddles, Taylor's *English Riddles;*[13] for rhymes and

11. Gavin Greig, *Last Leaves of Traditional Ballads and Ballad Airs*, ed. Alex. Keith (Aberdeen, 1925).

12. Antti Aarne and Stith Thompson, *The Types of the Folk-Tale*, FFC 74 (Helsinki, 1928). A new revised and enlarged edition, FFC 184, was published Helsinki, 1961.

13. Archer Taylor, *English Riddles from Oral Tradition* (Berkeley, 1951).

games, the books of Montgomerie,[14] Gomme,[15] and
Opie;[16] and for customs, beliefs, and superstitions, Gregor's
Folk-Lore of the North-East of Scotland.[17] In each case, I
added to the finding lists compiled for each genre the
items which I had collected from other informants and
had not found in any of the books used.

When using finding lists, collectors are sometimes concerned with the problem of potential "pump-priming,"
that is, the informant's taking the collector's cues as a
basis for creating items to please the collector or himself.
In most cases, a collector familiar with the materials of
the region should be able to judge whether the informant
is faking pieces. Actually, the collector who comes across
an informant capable of creating items on the spot is in a
fortunate position, for he may be able to study the very
manner in which new folklore is created. Even in faking
materials, the informant is forced to draw on traditional
themes, commonplaces, forms, content, and structures
which are known to him. The folklore fakers among a
collector's informants are to be encouraged rather than
discouraged, for through them some of the most intriguing
problems in folklore scholarship may be answered. It is,
of course, better if the informant indicates when he is
creating materials and when he is simply repeating
materials as a link in the chain of tradition. The best
assurance of an informant's complete honesty in this
matter is the high regard with which he views his relation
to the collector. Once the informant understands and

14. Nora and William Montgomerie, *Scottish Nursery Rhymes* (London, 1946), and *Sandy Candy and other Scottish Nursery Rhymes* (London,
1948).

15. Alice B. Gomme, *The Traditional Games of England, Scotland and
Ireland*. 2 vols. (London, 1894, 1898, reprinted New York, 1964).

16. Iona and Peter Opie, *The Lore and Language of Schoolchildren*
(Oxford, 1959).

17. Rev. Walter Gregor, *Notes on the Folk-Lore of the North-East of
Scotland* (London, 1881).

appreciates the value of the collector's work and the importance of his own fidelity in supplying information, the collector will be in a position to recite entire pieces without fear that the informant will later repeat them and claim them as part of his repertory.

Though a collector may use finding lists in an attempt to uncover the total repertory of an informant, he should be advised that it is impossible to do so. Working intensively with one family for almost a year, and utilizing every method known to me, including the use of long and detailed finding lists, I was still able to collect numerous items from them on my last day in their company; and even at the time of this writing (four years since I last saw them) I still receive letters from them regularly in which they send along folklore materials which they had been unable to recall when I was collecting from them. Since no finding list can be complete, its use will not guarantee the obtaining of an informant's total repertory; it will, however, bring him closer to that goal than he might have come without it.

CHAPTER IX

Motivation and Remuneration of Informants

NON-COLLECTORS usually are surprised by the size of a field worker's haul of songs and stories. It seems incredible to them that relative strangers are willing to spend so much time with, and give so much of themselves to, a collector. "What is it," they want to know, "that motivates an informant to reach into his memory and reveal materials and data which are so intricately and personally bound up with his life?"

There is no simple answer to the question. The problem of motivating informants is dependent upon the theoretical frame of reference of the collector and the type of field project undertaken by him.

1. Transient Collecting

The travelling collector staying only a few days in any one place or community, collecting from hundreds of informants, making casual relationships, getting a story in a barbershop here or on a bus there, listening to a boarding house session or exchanging jokes in a bar, need not particularly concern himself with the problem of motivating informants. For him, "collecting is very much a matter of timing, chance, and circumstance."[1]

But the collector who works as a transient collects transient folklore—the stories casually related to casual acquaintances and strangers. Much of the folklore of America is of that order because modern America is so large, so busy, so impersonal that there is less and less place outside of the home for deep relationships. For the transient collector the job is a relatively simple one because he has to concern himself only with making acquaintances, not with plumbing the depths of human beings. People like to talk, to be listened to; they need an audience, and the travelling collector, taking full advantage of his cloak of anonymity, of his "stranger value," satisfies that need. One of my North Carolina informants, who is visited by four or five transient collectors every summer, has verbalized a philosophy which is perhaps typical of the attitude with which such collectors are viewed:

> Tell him a story or two, talk to him friendly like . . . it don't cost anything to talk to a stranger. In your life one minute and out the next. You make him feel good 'cause he got what he came for, and you got a few laughs out of it, too, so why not cooperate . . . it don't cost anything.[2]

Rarely will the travelling collector have to concern himself with the problem of remunerating his informants. The stories and beliefs recited to the collector come from the informant's need to express himself and the availability of the collector as an auditor. The casual meeting can be followed with an invitation to share a meal or a drink

1. Richard M. Dorson, *Bloodstoppers and Bearwalkers: Folk Traditions of the Upper Peninsula* (Cambridge, Mass., 1952), p. 4.

2. Notes on conversation with J. F., singer, storyteller, and salesman (now retired), made in Asheville, N. C,, Summer, 1956.

with the collector, or the informant may invite the collector to visit his home. In a small town, the informant may be mindful of the status which such a visit may give him in the eyes of his neighbors, or he may simply be seeking approval or recognition from someone outside his own small social circle. Usually a chance to hear his own voice played back on the collector's sound recorder will more than serve as an incentive to further cooperation on his part. But the collector will rarely be able to find out what that informant's stories or songs mean to him, because to do that the field worker would have to collect the man as well as his folklore. And the transient collector, simply by fact of the nature of his project, will not have the time to get to know the man himself.

2. Psychological Gratification

The preceding advice is not meant to denigrate the important work of the travelling collector. Most relationships are casual, and the folklore passed on in the course of such relationships is a vital factor in the chain of tradition. However, the major contributions to our knowledge of tradition and its processes must come from the collector who works intensively with its core—the individual tradition bearer, his family, and his community. During the early days of his stay in a community, the field worker may take full advantage of his "stranger value," and the first few stories, songs, riddles, and beliefs will come easily once he has learned to press the right buttons. But the motivation necessary to start an informant is considerably less than that necessary to keep him going, to make him reveal what lies beneath the surface.

There is nothing mystical about such motivation. It is made up of equal amounts of conscious effort on the part of the collector to set up the proper kinds of relationships and his own natural ability and willingness to become involved in the life of his informants.

At the conscious level, motivation may be structured or manipulated in several ways. The collector, for example, may make calculated appeals to the pride of his informant. While the motivating inspiration behind a collector's work—advancing the cause of folklore as a discipline—is rarely the same incentive which inspires an informant to cooperate, he may be motivated by an interest in preserving the folklore of his community or nation, a quasi-scientific interest which he shares with the collector. Collectors in Ireland, for example, have found that "the country people seem to realize instinctively that we are doing something important for them, and that for the first time people have come to them to write the traditions which have been handed down from their forefathers."[3] I found the same situation existing in Scotland where national pride in native speech and traditions enables a collector to probe ever deeper into the folklore of a community.

Though perhaps not so important a motivating factor as in our own society, the possibility that a collector will bring some small portion of fame to an informant by publishing his name and materials may serve as a strong incentive. An informant's ego drive may well be made to serve the collector's needs by the promise that his songs, his tales, and perhaps even his photograph will be included in the field worker's publication of collectanea. But the collector who makes that kind of promise must be sure that he intends to keep it. The promise cannot be simply a device to get the informant to reveal his materials and his life story.

3. Statement made by Seán Ó Súilleabháin in *Four Symposia on Folklore*, ed. Stith Thompson, Indiana Univ. Folklore Series No. 8 (Bloomington, 1953), p. 14.

Where the collector has singled out one star performer or a family for an intensive study, he may play on the informants' pride in having been so chosen. Of the many potential individuals who could have been selected, the collector thought only one informant or family was worth concentrating his efforts upon. Informants chosen in this manner then feel bound to prove to the collector that he has made no mistake. They will usually respond by giving the collector all the time and attention he needs, will rack their memories to dig up almost everything which they ever knew, heard, or experienced, and will generally go out of their way to prove their status as prime sources.

Perhaps the best incentives to cooperation with a collector develop from his having created the proper kind of rapport. By participating as fully and as naturally as possible in the activities of the community and by a consistent pattern of socializing with informants, the collector is able to work toward creating the kind of deep relationship which will permit him to obtain the full confidence of his informants. The only real incentive to an informant for allowing the collector to probe deeply is the mutual regard which the two eventually develop. This regard does not spring up overnight; it is a slow and gradual process, developing out of the conscious effort on the part of the collector to establish rapport, but at some point becoming a non-motivated, unconscious, and genuine involvement with the people with whom the collector lives. In so far as we can consciously rationalize, and therefore describe, its elements, the essence of this involvement is sharing. There need never be any question of rewarding the informant at this level because the relationship is rewarding in itself. The informant comes to feel valued as a person, not just as a source of data, to know that he is talking to someone who is sympathetic as well as curious.[4]

4. Benjamin D. Paul, "Interview Techniques and Field Relationships" in *Anthropology Today*, ed. A. L. Kroeber (Chicago, 1953), p. 445.

The collector, too, has problems which his informants want (and perhaps need) to share, and the two exchange roles, with the collector satisfying the curiosity of his informants. When you confide in people you get confidence back.[5] The confidences exchanged must be scrupulously guarded; only if they remain the private knowledge of the informant and his collector-confidant can there be a base on which additional and ever deeper confidences will be built. By the exchange of jokes, reminiscences, songs, personal services, specialized knowledge, confidences, happiness, and sadness, the collecting of folklore becomes part of a much larger experience—the formation of deep human relationships. Through it the field worker comes to collect more than folklore; he also collects the people who create, shape, and transmit it.

The scientist in us warns that "motivation through personal bonds is a two-edged sword. It may result in over-motivation and in the observer's renunciation of detachment."[6] But the scientific collector is also a human being, and his greatest value to his discipline is the fact that he is not an electronic computor which classifies and categorizes and comes up with non-human (and frequently anti-human) responses and solutions. The collector feels and senses things, and this is as important as seeing and reporting only facts. Because of his scientific training he is able to separate the facts from his feelings when his analysis calls for that, or to mix them in various proportions when that is called for, and is thereby enabled to solve the essentially human problems involved in the processes of folklore. Nor should the scientific collector ever feel that he has to deny (even to himself) the love and high regard which he has for his informants as friends and people.

5. Alan Lomax in *Four Symposia,* p. 85.
6. Clyde Kluckhohn, "The Personal Document in Anthropological Science" in *The Use of Personal Documents in History, Anthropology, and Sociology,* Social Science Research Council Bull. 53 (New York, 1945), p. 119.

> . . . the very thing which forces us to examine, which forces us to wish to know everything, without flinching about our people—the very thing which forces us to intensive and so far as possible objective studies, the very thing which makes us clear-headed at evaluating—is that deep loving regard which we have.[7]

Indeed, the collector who is incapable of becoming involved with his informants, of developing a "deep loving regard" for them, had best restrict his collecting to transient folklore (which has its own importance). It is impossible to get more out of a relationship than one is willing to put into it. The collector who wishes to come to grips with the essence of the folklore process, with its meaning and motivation, must be able to get below the surface and to know the inner man. This he can do only by becoming deeply involved with that inner man.

3. Material Inducements

We have thus far referred only to those inducements or incentives which involve the psychological gratification of informants in motivating them to full cooperation with the field worker. Also to be considered are those inducements involving the material gain of informants. Lumped together under the heading of material gain are monetary payments, gifts, non-financial assistance, and drinking.

Monetary Payments

Notes and Queries on Anthropology recommends that ". . . it is inadvisable to pay directly for information.

7. Samuel P. Bayard in *Four Symposia,* p. 167.

The best plan is to ascertain the amount which a man normally earns in following his usual occupation—or, if he has no paid occupation, the amount which would recompense him for the loss of a day's work—and make this the basis of payment."[8] This is sound advice, but should apply only to informants whose actual working time is taken up by the collector. Usually a collector will be able to work with informants during the hours after their work day is over, and this is preferable to taking them away from gainful employment of any kind. However, survey collectors and others who are unable to spread their interviewing and collecting sessions over several evenings may be forced to ask certain informants to take time off from their jobs. In such cases the collector should avoid giving the informant the impression that his information or materials are being purchased, but rather should indicate that he is being recompensed for earnings lost during the time he spends with the collector.

Payment in such cases should always be in terms of the informant's economic system.[9] If a man's wages in a specific country comes to the equivalent of $1.00 a day, then the collector should pay him at that rate, not at the rate which a performer might be paid in America. "Too large a remuneration . . . is likely to arouse suspicion and give the impression that the material is of marketable value."[10] And, too, there is always the chance that in some highly individualistic societies over-generous payment may actually result in the collector buying contempt for himself rather than obtaining information or materials.[11]

8 *Notes and Queries on Anthropology*, Sixth Edition (London, 1951), p. 44.

9. Ralph Piddington, *An Introduction to Social Anthropology*, Vol. II (Edinburgh, 1957), p. 556.

10. Maud Karpeles and Arnold Baké, *Manual for Folk Music Collectors*, International Folk Music Council (London, 1951), p. 9.

11. Piddington, Vol. II, p. 556.

In those societies in which folklore is performed by professionals, payment should be made only at the rates they normally receive for their services. Non-professional traditional bearers should be offered pay only when they are required to take time off from gainful employment.

At times the collector will meet people who will refuse payment even when their cooperation means the loss of potential income. The successful farmer, for example, may not mind the loss of income-producing time and will be too proud to accept payment for it. However, the collector should not take undue advantage of this situation and should restrict work-time sessions only to those instances when evening or after-hours sessions are out of the question.

The collector will occasionally be faced with a situation in which previous collectors have already set a pattern of paying informants. Where this occurs as the result of a still-continuing collecting project or one sponsored by a government or national cultural body, the collector will usually be obliged to follow the precedent. Should he have the money to do so, he should then make payments at the going rates set by the previous collectors; but if the collector's funds are not sufficient to permit payment of informants, then at the time he establishes his role in the community he should also make that clear. Usually there will be little resistance to cooperating with the collector once the situation has been made clear to the inhabitants. Once this pattern is set, however, the collector must be consistent, for to make exceptions and pay some informants while refusing pay to others may result in his losing the cooperation of both parties.

"In some countries and regions, the payment of money will be refused and the pride of the informants may be wounded if it is offered."[12] For this reason it is usually

12. Karpeles and Baké, p. 9.

better to avoid offering payment except in cases in which the informants are losing money through otherwise being employed. If, however, an unemployed person, such as a housewife, elderly or retired person, or an invalid, requests payment, then his or her request should be satisfied unless the collector has already established a pattern of non-payment. In some countries (for example Jamaica), a pattern of payment-expectation for all services to strangers is so well established that the collector can be sure he will receive little cooperation without payments being made to his informants.[13]

Even when payments are made to informants, the collector must not be deluded into believing that he is obtaining the full cooperation of those individuals. The payment of money usually will insure nothing more than their cooperation to the degree which they feel constitutes a fair return for the collector's money. Rarely will this include the self-analysis and dramatic disclosures for which the collector's probing may call. The paid informant will need the additional incentives of psychological gratification before he will permit the collector to probe deeply; and this can be bought only at the price of personal involvement on the part of the collector in the lives of his informants.

Gifts

Some collectors have suggested giving informants gifts when it is obvious that they will not accept payment. However, a proud person may see through this as merely another attempt at making payment. When a gift is given, it should be done in such a manner that the informant is unaware that he is accepting it as such. George Pullen Jackson used to carry around several bags of tobacco,

13. Information from personal conversation with Dr. MacEdward Leach, March 8, 1963.

which he then fobbed off on an informant by indicating that he really didn't have any use for all of it and would the informant be good enough to relieve him of some of it.[14]

Most collectors, however, prefer to send their informants gifts at Christmas time or after they have left the field. Here, too, the collector should be careful that his motives are not misconstrued and that his informants recognize his gifts as being from a friend and not simply as delayed payment for services rendered to an impersonal collector.

In any case, the gift sent after the collector has left the field can have no affect on the informant during the field trip itself and so cannot be viewed as an incentive for motivating the cooperation of the informant. It may, however, result in that informant cooperating with later collectors or with the first collector, should he return for further work in that area. Whatever the circumstances, the motivating force behind the giving of the gift should be one of good will and friendship and never be thought of in terms of a payment or incentive.

Non-Financial Assistance

Perhaps the greatest service which the collector can perform for an informant, and which may serve to motivate the latter towards greater cooperation, is personal assistance at various levels. The Irish Folklore Commission, for example, helps its informants in many ways, including obtaining radio sets and pensions for the blind, getting jobs for the children of informants, and helping to cut governmental red tape when necessary.[15] The individual collector may not be in a position to assist in any of these ways, but he can write letters for his inform-

14. George P. Jackson in *Four Symposia*, p. 18.
15. Seán O Súilleabháin in *Four Symposia*, p. 13.

ants, obtain things for them when they are unable to obtain them for themselves, or act in their behalf when requested to do so. One service which the collector can perform to good advantage to himself as well is to hire an informant or his children to assist with transcribing materials or notes, to decipher dialect and explain obscure localisms, or generally to act as clerical assistants. The individual is hired at the going rate or after a fair and mutual agreement is reached. But whatever service the collector performs, it must be carried out in the good will of a general system of mutual aid and reciprocity between two good friends.

Liquor

Though rarely mentioned in print, many collectors readily admit to using alcoholic beverages to induce their informants to perform for them or give them information. Rather than acting as an incentive, however, one suspects that its primary value is as a stimulant without which many informants may be unable to perform effectively. But whether it is intended as an incentive or used as a stimulant, the collector must keep in mind the possibility that the use of alcohol at a collecting session may end with that session becoming a drinking bout. In working with informants who have shown little ability to hold their liquor, it is usually better to keep liquor out of a collecting session so that both collector and informant can maintain full awareness during the session itself. The proper time to drink socially with such informants is after a session is over, when a bottle can be opened or a trip made to the nearest bar or pub and good friends can get roaring drunk together if they care to.

Sometimes the question of introducing liquor into a collecting session is brought up by the informants, especially when liquor is expensive or difficult to get and the informants are getting on in years. They may then refer to it euphemistically as a "tonic" or "throat medicine" with the impression given to the collector that they really can't sing or tell a story without first wetting their throats. Here liquor serves the double role of incentive and stimulant, and should the collector decide to satisfy his informants' thirst, he would do well to reserve control of the bottle for himself, doling out drinks at a rate at which both he and his informants can continue to function properly.[16]

*   *   *

Whatever form of remuneration or incentive a collector applies to the problem of motivating his informants, he is bound to keep in mind that it should not be a one-way process, and that the best motivational inducements are those in which an equal exchange takes place. Perhaps the best statement of this striving for equality in the exchange relationship is Alan Lomax's comment during a symposium on collecting at the Midcentury International Folklore Conference at Indiana University in 1950:

> People say to me that they would like to help me along with my work, that I look as if I needed help. And I tell them that I am taking up their time and that I would like to make it up to them. There was never any question of dignity being

16. My comments on the use of liquor as means of motivating informants do not refer to those situations or contexts in which performance is directly connected with the consumption of alcoholic beverages. For example, the collector who plies his informants with liquor on New Year's Eve is playing a normal social role. MacEdward Leach, in conversation with me on March 22, 1963, told of the almost continuous state of partial inebriation of his Newfoundland informants during the period between Christmas and Twelfth Night; at such times they performed songs and stories never heard at other times of the year. The collector utilizing liquor in such a context is both a good neighbor and a good collector, whatever his specific motivation for its use may be at the time.

involved; none of us in our situation was more dignified than anyone else. If the informant liked to drink, I drank, and if he liked to acquire a salary, I haggled with him very hard and very seriously, but we fought over it as equals.[17]

Any feeling of inequality in such an exchange may result in antagonism or guilt feelings, depending upon the direction in which the inequality is weighted, with a concomitant loss of rapport. And it is upon rapport with our informants, more than anything else, that we are dependent if we are to achieve success in the field.

17. Alan Lomax in *Four Symposia,* p. 20.

AFTERWORD

By the time the reader has made his way to this *Afterword*, he has probably become aware of two limitations of the present work beyond those stated in the *Foreword*.

First, as a *Guide* to collecting methods to be used in field work, this book is valid only for American and Western European folklore traditions. (To the degree to which it has been based on my own field experiences, it may actually be valid only for certain regions of the United States and one corner of Western Europe). However, since the present work has also been based in part on the reported methods of ethnographers and field workers in other disciplines in various parts of the world, I suspect that it may prove generally applicable among other nations and peoples.

Second, and again to the degree to which they are based on my own field work in Anglo-American communities, the methods described in this *Guide* are directed mainly at collecting folklore which has passed the peak of vitality and is less vital than one might find in folk communities in other parts of the world. The Western folklorist must dig for his treasures, covered over as they are by the products of modern mass communications media and mass production methods which have contributed to the destruction of traditional ways of living. In parts of Eastern Europe, Africa, Asia Minor and the Far East, there are folk communities where lore is the whole of life and the amount of folklore is more or less infinite; the collector in such communities is surrounded by folklore and the gold he seeks requires little if any digging. However, while folklore materials lie on or close to the surface, the field worker must still search for the inner man behind the folklore, and the present work will therefore prove valid for describing the methods to be used in obtaining data which cannot simply be scooped up with a collector's shovel.

Both of these limitations point strongly to the need for numerous field guides based entirely on work in specific areas of the world. Every nation and peoples have their own folklore, modes of expression, and behavior patterns in the use and meaning of folklore. It follows that every community presents problems which are unique for that community and which no general methodology can hope to cover with any degree of thoroughness. It will be the job of folklore collectors in all areas of the world to report their field methods in detail. Their contributions in this regard may be more important to the status of folklore as an academic discipline than the folklore materials and data which they garner in the course of their field work.

BIBLIOGRAPHY

AA. See *American Anthropologist*.

Aarne, Antti, and Stith Thompson. *The Types of the Folk-tale*. FFC 74, Helsinki, 1928. Revised and enlarged edition, FFC 184, Helsinki, 1961.

Abrahams, Roger D. *Negro Folklore from South Philadelphia: A Collection and Analysis*. Philadelphia, 1962. (Unpublished dissertation.)

Ackerknecht, E. H. "On the Collection of Data Concerning Primitive Medicine," *AA* 47 (1945), 427-431.

Addy, S. O. "The Collection of Folklore," *Folk-Lore* 13 (1902), 297-299.

American Anthropologist. Old Series, Washington, 1888-1898. New Series, Washington, 1899-. (Referred to as *AA*.)

Anthropology Today: An Encyclopedic Inventory. Prepared under the chairmanship of A. L. Kroeber. Chicago, 1953.

An Appraisal of Anthropology Today, eds. Sol Tax, Loren C. Eiseley, Irving Rouse, and C. F. Voeglin. Chicago, 1953.

Asadowskij, Mark. *Eine sibrische Märchenerzählerin*. FFC 68, Helsinki, 1926.

Ball, John. "Style In the Folktale," *Folk-Lore* 65 (1954), 170-172.

Banks, M. Macleod. *British Calendar Customs: Orkney and Shetland.* London, 1946.

_____. *British Calendar Customs: Scotland.* 3 vols. London, 1937, 1939, 1941.

Bartlett, F., M. Ginsberg, E. J. Lindgren, and R. H. Thouless. *The Study of Society: Methods and Problems.* London, 1939.

Bascom, Wm. R. "Folklore and Anthropology," *JAF* 66 (1953), 283-290.

_____. "Four Functions of Folklore," *JAF* 67 (1954), 333-349.

Bauman, Richard. "Y. L. Cahan's Instructions on the Collecting of Folklore," *NYFQ* 18 (1962), 284-289.

_____. "The Collecting of Proverbs," *WF* 22 (1963), 271-272.

Bayard, Samuel P. "The Materials of Folklore," *JAF* 66 (1953), 1-17.

Beck, Horace P. "Say Something Dirty!" *JAF* 75 (1962), 195-199.

_____. (ed.) *Folklore In Action: Essays for Discussion in Honor of MacEdward Leach.* Philadelphia, 1962.

Bennett, J. W. "The Study of Cultures: A Survey of Technique and Methodology in Field Work," *American Sociological Review* 13 (1948), 672-689.

Botkin, B. A. *Supplementary Instructions to the American Guide Manual: Manual for Folklore Studies.* 1938.

Buchanan, R. H. "The Study of Folklore," *Ulster Folklife* 1 (1955), 8-12.

Burne, C. S. "The Collection of Folklore," *Folk-Lore* 13 (1902), 299-302.

_____. *The Handbook of Folklore.* London, 1914.

Charters, S. B. "Some Do's and Don't's of Field Recording," *Sing Out* 12, No. 3 (Summer, 1962), 49-53.

Chase, Richard. *American Folk Tales and Songs.* New York, 1956. Chapter 6, "American Collector's Guide," 228-235.

Clarke, Kenneth and Mary. *Introducing Folklore.* New York, 1963. "Collecting Folklore," 110-115.

Collins Jr., Fletcher. "An Aid to the Discovery of Folk Song: A List of Finders for Traditional Ballads, Songs and Play-Parties," *SFQ* 5 (1941), 235-250.

Colson, Elizabeth. "The Intensive Study of Small Sample Communities," *Method and Perspective in Anthropology,* ed. Robert F. Spencer. Minneapolis, 1954. 43-59.

Crooke, William. "The Collection of Folklore," *Folk-Lore* 13 (1902), 302-307.

Davis Jr., A. K. *Traditional Ballads of Virginia.* Cambridge, Mass., 1929.

——————. *More Traditional Ballads of Virginia.* Chapel Hill, 1960.

Degh, L. "Some Questions of the Social Function of Story-telling," *Acta Ethnographica* 7 (1957), 91-147.

Delargy, J. H. "The Gaelic Story-teller," *Proceedings of the British Academy* 31 (1945), 177-221.

Dollard, J. *Criteria for the Life History.* New Haven, 1935.

Dorson, Richard M. *Bloodstoppers and Bearwalkers: Folk Traditions of the Upper Peninsula.* Cambridge, Mass., 1952.

——————. "Collecting in County Kerry," *JAF* 66 (1953), 19-42.

——————. *Negro Tales in Michigan.* Cambridge, Mass., 1956.

——————. "Standards for Collecting and Publishing American Folktales," in "The Folktale: A Symposium," *JAF* 70 (1957), 53-57.

——————. Collecting Folklore in Jonesport, Maine, *Proceedings of the American Philosophical Society* 101 (1957), 270-289.

——————. "A Theory for American Folklore," *JAF* 72 (1959), 197-215.

——————. "Oral Styles of American Folk Narrators," *Style In Language,* ed. T. A Sebeok. Cambridge, Mass., 1960. 27-51. Reprinted in *Folklore in Action,* ed. Horace P. Beck, Philadelphia, 1962. 77-100.

——————. *Buying the Wind.* Chicago, 1964. Introduction, "Collecting Oral Folklore in the United States," 1-20.

Dundes, Alan. "On the Psychology of Collecting Folklore," *Tennessee Folklore Society Bulletin* 28 (1962), 65-74.

FFC. See *Folklore Fellows Communications.*

Fife, Austin and Alta. *Saints of Sage and Saddle.* Bloomington, Ind., 1956.

Fischer, J. L. "The Sociopsychological Analysis of Folktales," *Current Anthropology* 4 (1963), 235-295.

Folk-Lore. London, 1883- .

Folklore and Folk Music Archivist. Bloomington, Ind., 1958- .

Folklore Fellows Communications. Helsinki, 1910- . (Referred to as *FFC.*)

Gardner, Emelyn E. *Folklore from the Schoharie Hills, New York.* Ann Arbor, Mich., 1937.

Gardner, Emelyn E,. and Geraldine J. Chickering. *Ballads and Songs of Southern Michigan.* Ann Arbor, Mich., 1939.

Goddard, P. E. "The Relation of Folklore to Anthropology," *JAF* 28 (1915), 18-23.

Goldstein, Kenneth S. "Ghosts, Witches and the Devil in Northeast Scotland," *Fulbright Courier* (March, 1960), 19-24.

——————. "William Robbie: Folk Artist of the Buchan District, Aberdeenshire," *Folklore in Action,* ed. Horace P. Beck. Philadelphia, 1962. 101-111.

——————. "Riddling Traditions in Northeastern Scotland," *JAF* 76 (1963), 330-336.

——————. "The Collecting of Superstitious Beliefs," *Keystone Folklore Quarterly* 9, No. 1 (Spring, 1964), 13-22.

Gomme, Alice B. *The Traditional Games of England, Scotland and Ireland.* 2 vols. London, 1894, 1898. Reprinted New York, 1964.

Gomme, George L. *The Handbook of Folklore.* London, 1890.

Grainger, Percy. "Collecting With the Phonograph," *Journal of the Folk-Song Society* 3 (1908), 147-162.

Greenway, John. *Literature Among the Primitives.* Hatboro, Penna., 1964.

Gregor, Rev. Walter. *Notes on the Folk-Lore of the North-East of Scotland.* London, 1881.

Greig, Gavin. *Folk-Song of the North-East.* 2 vols. Peterhead, Aberdeenshire, 1909, 1914. Reprinted, together with *Folk-Song in Buchan,* Hatboro, Penna., 1963.

——————. *Last Leaves of Traditional Ballads and Ballad Airs Collected in Aberdeenshire,* ed. Alex. Keith. Aberdeen, 1925.

Grudde, Hertha. *Wie ich meine "Plattdeutschen Volksmärchen aus Ostpreussen" aufschrieb.* FFC 102, Helsinki, 1932.

Halpert, Herbert, in collaboration with George Herzog. *Folksong Questionnaire.* Joint Committee on Folk Arts, W.P.A., 1939.

Halpert, Herbert. "Truth in Folk-Songs," in John Harrington Cox, *Traditional Ballads Mainly from West Virginia.* National Service Bureau Publication No. 75-S. New York, 1939.

——————. "La técnica para la grabación de canciones folklóricas," *Boletín Latino-Americano de Música* 5 (1941), 177-183.

——————. "A Michigan Lumberjack Singer," *HF* 1 (1942), 81-84.

——————. "The Folksinger Speaks," *HF* 3 (1944), 29-35, 48-55.

——————. "The Functional Approach," in "Conference on the Character and State of Studies in Folklore," *JAF* 59 (1946), 510-512.

——————. "American Regional Folklore," in "Folklore Research in North America," *JAF* 60 (1947), 355-366.

——————. "Vitality of Tradition and Local Songs," *Journal of the International Folk Music Council* 3 (1951), 35-40.

——————. "Some Undeveloped Areas in American Folklore," *JAF* 70 (1957), 299-304.

——————. "Folklore: Breadth versus Depth," *JAF* 71 (1958), 97-103.

——————. "Folklore and Obscenity: Definition and Problems," *JAF* 75 (1962), 190-194.

Hand, Wayland D. *Popular Beliefs and Superstitions from North Carolina.* Vols. 6 and 7 of *The Frank C. Brown Collection of North Carolina Folklore.* Durham, N. C., 1961, 1964.

Harlow, F. P. *The Making of a Sailor or Sea Life Aboard a Yankee Square-Rigger.* Salem, Mass., 1928.

Hartland, E. S. *The Science of Fairy Tales.* London, 1891.

_____. *Welsh Folklore: Its Collection and Study.* Liverpool, (1893?)

Harvey, S. M. "A Preliminary Investigation of the Interview," *British Journal of Psychology* 28 (1938), 263-287.

Hedblom, Folke. "The Institute for Dialect and Folklore Research at Uppsala, Sweden," *The Folklore and Folk Music Archivist* 3, No. 4 (1961).

Herskovits, Melville J. "Folklore After 100 Years," *JAF* 59 (1946), 89-100.

_____. "The Hypothetical Situation: A Technique of Field Research," *Southwestern Journal of Anthropology* 6 (1950), 32-40.

_____. *Man and His Works.* New York, 1950.

_____. "Some Problems of Method in Ethnography," *Method and Perspective in Anthropology,* ed. R. F. Spencer. Minneapolis, 1954. 3-24.

Herskovits, Melville J. and Frances. *Dahomean Narrative: A Cross Cultural Analysis.* Evanston, Ill., 1958.

Herzog, George. *Research in Primitive and Folk Music in the United States.* American Council of Learned Societies Bulletin 24. Washington, 1936.

_____. "The Study of Folksong in America," *SFQ* 2 (1938), 59-64.

_____. "Song: Folk Song and the Music of Folk Song," Funk and Wagnall's *Standard Dictionary of Folklore, Mythology, and Legend,* eds. Maria Leach and Jerome Fried. Vol. 2. New York, 1950. 1032-1050.

HF. See *Hoosier Folklore.*

Hilger, Sister M. Inez. "An Ethnographic Field Method," *Method and Perspective in Anthropology,* ed. R. F. Spencer. Minneapolis, 1954. 25-42.

Hints to Collectors of Folk Music. Folk Song Society, London, n.d.

Hoosier Folklore. Bloomington, Ind., 1942-1950.

Hudson, A. P. *Folksongs of Mississippi and their Background*. Chapel Hill, 1936.

"The Irish Folklore Commission: A Sample Questionnaire," *The Folklore and Folk Music Archivist* 4, No. 2 (1961).

Jacobs, Joseph. "The Folk," *Folk-Lore* 4 (1893), 233-238.

Jacobs, Melville. "Folklore," *The Anthropology of Franz Boas*. San Francisco, 1959. 119-123.

_____. *The Content and Style of an Oral Literature*. Viking Fund Publications in Anthropology No. 26. New York, 1959.

JAF. See *Journal of American Folklore*.

Jahoda, Marie, Morton Deutsch, and Stuart W. Cook (eds.). *Research Methods in Social Relations*. 2 vols. New York, 1951.

Jansen, Wm. Hugh. "The Folksinger's Defense," *HF* 9 (1950), 65-70.

_____. "From Field to Library," *Folk-Lore* 63 (1952), 152-157.

_____. "Classifying Performance in the Study of Verbal Folklore," *Studies in Folklore in Honor of Stith Thompson*, ed. W. E. Richmond. Bloomington, Ind., 1957. 110-118.

Jones, Louis C. "A Student Guide to Collecting Folklore," *NYFQ* 2 (1946), 148-153.

Journal of American Folklore. Boston, New York, and Philadelphia, 1888-. (Referred to as *JAF*.)

Karpeles, Maud, and Arnold Baké. *Manual for Folk Music Collectors*. London, 1951.

Karpeles, Maud (ed.). *The Collecting of Folk Music and Other Ethnomusicological Material*. London, 1958. Revised edition of the Karpeles and Baké *Manual* above.

Kluckhohn, Clyde. "The Personal Document in Anthropological Science," *The Use of Personal Documents in History, Anthropology, and Sociology*, eds., Louis Gottschalk, Clyde Kluckhohn, and Robert Angell. Social Science Research Council Bulletin 53. New York, 1945. 79-173.

Kluckhohn, Florence. "The Participant-Observer Technique in Small Communities," *American Journal of Sociology* 46 (1940), 331-343.

Kornhauser, Arthur. "Constructing Questionnaires and Interview Schedules," *Research Methods in Social Relations*, ed. M. Jahoda et al. Vol. 2. New York, 1951. 423-462.

Leach, MacEdward. "Problems of Collecting Oral Literature," *Publications of the Modern Language Association* 77 (1962), 335-340.

Leach, MacEdward, and Tristram P. Coffin (eds.). *The Critics and the Ballad*. Carbondale, Ill., 1961.

Leach, Maria, and Jerome Fried (eds.). Funk and Wagnall's *Standard Dictionary of Folklore, Mythology, and Legend*. 2 vols. New York, 1949, 1950.

Legman, Gershon. *The Horn Book: Studies in Erotic Folklore and Bibliography*. New Hyde Park, New York, 1964.

Lewis, Oscar. "Controls and Experiments in Field Work," *Anthropology Today*. Chicago, 1953. 452-475.

Lindgren, E. J. "The Collection and Analysis of Folk-Lore," *The Study of Society: Methods and Problems*, ed. F. Bartlett et al., London, 1939. 328-378.

List, George. "Documenting Recordings," *The Folklore and Folk Music Archivist* 3, No. 3 (1960).

Lomax, Alan. "The Functional Aspects of Folklore," in "Conference on the Character and State of Studies in Folklore," *JAF* 59 (1946), 507-510.

——————. *Mister Jelly Roll*. New York, 1950.

——————. *The Rainbow Sign, A Southern Documentary*. New York, 1959.

——————. "Musical Style and Social Context," *AA* 61 (1959), 927-954.

——————. "Song Structure and Social Structure," *Ethnology* 1 (1962), 425-451.

Lomax, John A., and Alan Lomax. *Negro Folk Songs as Sung by Lead Belly*. New York, 1936.

Lomax, John A. "Field Experiences with Recording Machines," *SFQ* 1, No. 2 (June, 1937), 57-60.

——————. *Adventures of a Ballad Hunter*. New York, 1947.

Lord, Albert B. *The Singer of Tales*. Cambridge, Mass., 1960.

Lowie, R. H. *The History of Ethnological Theory*. New York, 1937.

Mackenzie, W. Roy. *The Quest of the Ballad.* Princeton, 1919.
Malinowski, Bronislaw. *Argonauts of the Western Pacific.* London, 1922.
––––––––––. *Myth in Primitive Psychology.* New York, 1926.
McAllester, David P. *Enemy Way Music.* Peabody Museum Papers 41, No. 3 (1954).
McLendon, A. L. "A Finding List of Play-Party Games," *SFQ* 8 (1944), 201-234.
McNeill, F. Marian. *The Silver Bough.* 3 vols. Glasgow, 1957, 1959, 1961.
McPherson, J. M. *Primitive Beliefs in the North-East of Scotland.* London, 1929.
Mead, Margaret. "More Comprehensive Field Methods," *AA* 35 (1933), 1-15.
Merriman, Alan P. "The Selection of Recording Equipment for Field Use," *Kroeber Anthropological Society Papers No. 10.* Berkeley, 1954. 5-9.
––––––––––. "Ethnomusicology: Discussion and Definition of the Field," *Ethnomusicology* 4 (1960), 107-114.
Montgomerie, Norah and William. *Scottish Nursery Rhymes.* London, 1946.
––––––––––. *Sandy Candy and other Scottish Nursery Rhymes.* London, 1948.
Morris, A. C. *Folksongs of Florida.* Gainesville, Florida, 1950.
Murdock, G. P. *Outline of Cultural Materials.* New Haven, 1950.
Murray, M. A. "England As a Field for Folklore Research," *Folk-Lore* 65 (1954), 1-9.
Nadel, S. F. "The Interview Technique in Social Anthropology," *The Study of Society: Methods and Problems,* ed. F. Bartlett et al., London, 1939. 317-327.
––––––––––. *The Foundations of Social Anthropology.* Glencoe, Ill., 1951.
Nettl, Bruno. "Recording Primitive and Folk Music in the Field," *AA* 56 (1954), 1101-1102.
––––––––––. *Theory and Method in Ethnomusicology.* Glencoe, Ill., 1964. Chapter 3, "Field Work," 62-97.

——————. *An Introduction to Folk Music in the United States.* Detroit, 1962. Chapter 9, "Collecting and Studying Folk Music," 75-84.

New York Folklore Quarterly. Ithaca, 1945- . (Referred to as *NYFQ.*)

Northrup, F. S. C. *The Logic of the Sciences and the Humanities.* New York, 1959.

Notes and Queries on Anthropology. 6th edition revised and rewritten by a Committee of the Royal Anthropological Institute of Great Britain and Ireland. London, 1951.

NYFQ. See *New York Folklore Quarterly.*

Ó Danachair, Caoimhín. "The Questionnaire System," *Bealoideas* 15 (1945), 203-217.

——————. "Irish Folk Narrative on Sound Records," *Laos* 1 (1951), 180-186.

——————. "The Irish Folklore Commission," *The Folklore and Folk Music Archivist 5,* No. 1 (1961).

Ó Súilleabháin, Séan. *A Handbook of Irish Folklore.* Dublin, 1942. Reprinted Hatboro, Pennsylvania, 1963.

Oeser, O. A. "The Value of Team Work and Functional Penetration as Methods in Social Investigation," *The Study of Society: Methods and Problems,* ed. F. Bartlett et al., London, 1939. 402-417.

Opie, Iona and Peter. *The Lore and Language of Schoolchildren.* Oxford, 1959.

Opie, Peter. "The Collection of Folklore in England," *Journal of the Royal Society of Arts* 101 (1953), 697-714.

Paul, Benj. D. "Interview Techniques and Field Relationships," *Anthropology Today.* Chicago, 1953. 430-451.

Piddington, Ralph. *An Introduction to Social Anthropology.* 2 vols. Edinburgh, 1950, 1957.

Randolph, Vance. *Ozark Folksongs.* 4 vols. Columbia, Mo., 1946, 1948, 1949, 1950.

Richards, A. I. "The Development of Field Work Methods in Social Anthropology," *The Study of Society: Methods and Problems,* ed. F. Bartlett et al. London, 1939. 272-316.

Richmond, W. Edson, (ed.). *Studies in Folklore in Honor of Stith Thompson*. Indiana Univ. Folklore Series No. 9. Bloomington, Ind., 1957.

Ritchie, Jean. *Singing Family of the Cumberlands*. New York, 1955.

Roberts, Leonard W. *Up Cutshin and Down Greasy: Folk-Ways of a Kentucky Mountain Family*. Lexington, 1959.

Rogers, C. "The Non-Directive Method as a Technique for Social Research," *American Journal of Sociology* 50 (1945), 279-283.

Rowe, J. H. "Technical Aids in Anthropology," *Anthropology Today*. Chicago, 1953. 895-940.

Sachs, Kurt. *The Wellsprings of Music*. The Hague, 1962.

Sackett, S. J., and Wm. E. Koch. *An Instructional Manual for Members of the Kansas Folklore Society*. Hays, Kansas, 1958.

Saslow, G., and E. D. Chapple. "A New Life-History Form with Instructions for Its Use," *Applied Anthropology* 4 (1945), 1-18.

Scarborough, Dorothy. *From a Southern Porch*. New York, 1919.

————. *A Song Catcher in Southern Mountains*. New York, 1937.

Seeger, Charles. "Professionalism and Amateurism in the Study of Folk Music," *JAF* 62 (1949), 107-113. Reprinted in *The Critics and the Ballad*, eds. MacEdward Leach and T. P. Coffin. Carbondale, Ill., 1961. 151-160.

Seligmann, C. G. "The Collection of Folklore," *Folk-Lore* 13 (1902), 310-312.

SFQ. See *Southern Folklore Quarterly*.

Sharp, Cecil J. *English Folk-Songs from the Southern Appalachians*, ed. Maud Karpeles. 2 vols. London, 1932.

Sheatsley, Paul B. "The Art of Interviewing and a Guide to Interviewer Selection and Training," *Research Methods in Social Relations*, ed. M. Jahoda et al. Vol. 2. New York, 1951. 463-492.

Skeat, Walter. "The Collection of Folklore," *Folk-Lore* 13 (1902), 307-310.

Sokolov, Y. M. *Russian Folklore*. trans. C. R. Smith. New York, 1950.

Southern Folklore Quarterly. Gainesville, Florida, 1937-. (Referred to as *SFQ*.)

Spencer, Robt. F., (ed.). *Method and Perspective in Anthropology*. Minneapolis, 1954.

von Sydow, C. W. "On the Spread of Tradition," *Selected Papers on Folklore*. Copenhagen, 1948. 11-43.

Taylor, Archer. "Some Trends and Problems in Studies of the Folk-Tale," *Studies in Philosophy* 37 (1940), 1-25.

——————. *English Riddles from Oral Tradition*. Berkeley, 1951.

Thomas, Lowell. *Tall Stories: The Rise and Triumph of the Great American Whopper*. New York, 1945.

Thompson, Stith. "American Folklore after Fifty Years," *JAF* 51 (1938), 1-9.

——————. "Folktale Collecting in Ireland," *SFQ* 2 (1938), 53-58.

——————. *The Folktale*. New York, 1946.

——————. "Advances in Folklore Studies," *Anthropology Today*. Chicago, 1953. 578-596.

——————. (ed). *Four Symposia on Folklore*. Indiana Univ. Folklore Series No. 8. Bloomington, Ind., 1953.

Vansina, J. "Recording the Oral History of the Bakuba — I. Methods," *Journal of African History* 1 (1960), 45-53.

Western Folklore. Continuation of *California Folklore Quarterly*. Berkeley and Los Angeles, 1942-. (Referred to as *WF*.)

WF. See *Western Folklore*.

Whyte, Wm. F. "Observational Field-work Methods," *Research Methods in Social Relations*, ed. M. Jahoda et al., Vol. 2. New York, 1951. 493-513.

Wilgus, D. K. *Anglo-American Folksong Scholarship Since 1898*. New Brunswick, N. J., 1959.

Wisser, Wilhelm. *Auf der Märchensuche*. Hamburg, [1926].

Wright, A. R. *British Calendar Customs: England*, ed. T. E. Lones. 3 vols. London, 1936, 1938, 1940.

Yankovíc, L. S. *Instructions for Collecting Material Regarding Folk Dances*. Belgrade, 1940.

INDEX

Aarne, Antti, 157n
Abrahams, Roger D., xviii, 129n
accessibility to informants, 48-49, 125
active tradition bearers, 63, 65-66
Afterword, 175-176
age groups, 72, 83, 150
alternate problems, 22, 27, 52
amateur collectors, viii, x, xv, 4, 9, 14, 16, 37
amateur folklorist, definition, 3n, 9
American Folklore Society, xv, xviii
analysis, 2, 6n, 44, 75, 123-124, 134, 154n
Anderson, Walter, 151n
anthropological folklorists, xiv, 4, 8, 10, 19
anthropologists, vii, xiii-xv, 4-5, 6, 7, 11, 19, 27, 37, 54, 77, 79n, 96, 116

Appalachians, field work in, xvi, 18, 53
applied folklorists, 2n
archives, 10, 41, 143, 154
area selected for field work, 21
audience, 83, 84, 85, 86, 107, 115-116, 128, 161
available literature, 37-39
average informants, 125
Azadovsky, M. K., 122n

Baké, Arnold, 167n, 168n
Ball, John, 98
Banks, M. Macleod, 29n
Bascom, William, 8
Bauman, Richard, 45n, 137n
Bayard, Samuel P., x, xviii, 166n
Beck, Horace P., 59n
beliefs, 52, 66, 68, 114, 116, 117, 120, 133, 151, 158, 161, 162 (also see *customs*, and *superstitions*)

bibliography, preparation of, 38
Boas, Franz, 8
boasts, 26
Botkin, Benjamin J., 61n, 116n
breadth collecting, 25n
Brittany, field work in, 19
Buckley, Bruce, xvii
Burne, Charlotte S., 5n, 10

Cahan, Y. L., 45n, 137n
calendar customs, 29, 69, 81, 83, 90
California, University of, 7n
Canada, field work in, 18
carbon copies, 143
case history of materials, 138-142
casual collecting, 63, 66, 160-162
change in role, 56
change, studies in, 33, 107, 134
Charters, Samuel B., 45n
Chase, Richard, 156n
checking interview data (see controls and checks)
Chickering, G. J., 62n
children as aids to collecting, 11, 55-56, 67, 72, 90, 150-154
children as bearers of adult traditions, 151, 154
children's folklore, 24, 67, 129-130, 147, 150-154
child-bearing beliefs, 56
Christmas gifts, 170

circumstances of interview, 120-121, 139
chunk commentary, 119, 123, 124
Coffin, Tristram P., xv, xvii
collecting projects, typology of, 24-26
collector-informant context, 86, 94, 128, 129
collector-performers, 44-45, 130-131, 150
Collins, Fletcher, 156n
Columbia University, xv
communications media, 32, 133, 136, 140, 144-150, 176
comparative folklorists, 2n, 3, 4-5
confidences, 165
conspicuousness of collector, 48, 50, 51
contacting collectors, 39-40, 46
contacting local folk, 39, 40-41, 49, 59
content analysis, 23
contexts, artificial, 80, 82, 84-85, 89, 90, 94, 98n, 127; formal, 81, 83; informal, 70, 81, 84, 127; natural, 70, 73, 78, 80-81, 82-83, 86, 87, 88, 90, 97, 101, 127; physical, 18, 23, 91, 114, 120; semi-formal, 81, 84, 90, 127; social, 18, 23, 70, 92, 115-116, 120
continuous residence, 33
control pitch, 43
controls and checks, 96, 112-115, 120

Cook, Stuart W., 76n, 82n, 109n, 111n, 112n, 113n
Cray, Ed, xvii
cultural anthropologists, xiii, 2n, 3, 6, 8, 10
customs, 52, 56, 114, 158 (also see *calendar customs*)

deception, 33, 57-59
depth collecting, 25, 28, 29, 48, 63, 64, 118, 134, 155, 161
Deutsch, Morton, 76n, 82n, 109n, 111n, 112n, 113n
devil beliefs, 68n, 115, 117, 147
dialect (see *language*)
Dick, James C., viii
direct questions, 109, 111, 127
directive interview, 110-111
discovering traditions, 18, 71
doctors, 35, 40, 55, 66
documentary, radio and television, 149
Dorson, Richard M., 2n, 8, 19, 54, 57n, 63n, 122n, 161n
dramatic disclosures (see *traumatic disclosures*)
drinking with informants, 69, 161, 166, 171-172, 173
duplication of efforts, 37, 39-40
duration of field trip (see *time considerations*)
duration of interview, 118-119

economy, 37, 167
education of informants, 37

educational affiliation, 53, 145
ego of informants, 58, 163
England, 29n, 158n
episodic works, 122-123, 124, 125
equipment, 34, 41-44, 45, 51, 96-103, 119-120, 124, 128-130, 137-138, 142-143; repairs to, 34, 43
Erixon, S., 155n
erotica (see *obscene folklore*)
Estonia, 151n
ethnographic approach, xiv, 7-8, 9, 10, 47
"ethnographic dynamite," 116-117, 128, 130
Europe, 10
evaluation, 2, 3, 75
exact transcription, 132-133, 154
experience in collecting, 32-33, 36, 49, 73, 101, 134, 157
expressive interview, 124

factionalism, 73
faking by informants, 158-159
farming, 68
fatigue, 31, 118
favor granting, 74
Fewkes, Jesse, 99
fidelity of recordings, 44
field experiments, 131, 151
field problems, kinds of, 23
field work, definition, x, 9n
field workers vs. library workers, 2n-3n
Fife, Alta and Austin, 96n

films, 41, 42, 97
finding lists, 108, 156-159
financial arrangements, 27, 28, 168
"first foot," 69
flattery, 52, 164
folk aesthetic, 4, 23, 69, 78, 106, 112, 137-138, 140
folk community, definition, 10
folk dance, 5
folk-life collectors, 11
folk medicine, 66, 67
folk music, 5
folk museums, 11, 154
folk newspapers, 148
folk religionists, 2n
folklore data, kinds of, 22-23, 37, 41
folklore, definition, 1-2, 5n, 10n, 11, 17n, 134-135
folklore fakers, 158-159
Folklore Institute, xv
folklore, use of term, 1, 52, 57
folklorists, kinds of, 2
folksong, 2n, 24, 44, 52, 54, 60, 63, 66, 69, 70, 83, 85, 86, 87n, 98n, 99, 112, 127, 130, 145, 146, 147, 151, 153, 157, 162, 163, 165, 172
folktale, 3, 4, 5n, 21, 24 26, 44, 52, 54, 60, 63, 64, 69, 70, 78, 81, 83, 86, 87n, 98, 99, 120, 127, 130, 145, 146, 147, 151, 153, 157, 160, 162, 163, 165, 172
follow-up interviews, 79, 96, 113-114, 121, 124
food supplies, 37, 65, 66

Foreword, xiii-xviii
formal social functions, 67
Fowke, Edith, xvii
Fried, Jerome, 1n
functional approach, 6n, 8, 15
fuel supplies, 65, 66
Fulbright Act, xv, 28
funds, 28

games, 60, 129-130, 153, 158
Gardner, Emelyn E., 55n, 62n
generalized acceptance, 56, 65, 79, 80
geography, 37
Germany, 154
gestures, 4, 86, 99
ghosts, 68n
gifts, 166, 169-170
Goldstein, Kenneth S., vii-xi, 68n, 89n, 122n, 133n
Gomme, Alice B., 158n
Gomme, George L., 5n, 10, 17n, 156n
Goodenough, Ward, xv, xvii
gossip, 55, 66, 67
government official, role of, 40, 53-54, 55n
graduate work, xv
Greenway, John, xviii, 10n
Gregor, Walter, 68n, 158n
Greig, Gavin, viii, ix, 146, 148n, 157n
"Gudeman's Croft," 68

Hallowell, A. Irving, xv
Halpert, Herbert, xvii, xviii, 7, 10n, 13n, 25n, 59n, 120n, 126n, 139n

Hand, Wayland D., 133n
handbooks, 5, 9, 11, 156
Harlow, Frederick P., 122n
health hazards, 34, 35
Henderson, Hamish, vii-xi,
  xvi, xvii, xviii, 39n
Herskovits, Melville J., 8,
  21, 27n, 29n, 30n, 31n, 33n,
  57n, 96n, 111n
Herzog, George, 10n, 120n,
  126n, 139n
historian, role of, 54
historic-geographic method, 3
historical reconstruction, 23,
  107, 114
Hoffman, Frank, xvii
Hogmanay, 69
homogeneous community, 32,
  50
"Horseman's Word," 68, 83
housing (see *selection of
  residence*)
humanism, 2, 58
humidity, 34
husband-wife teams, 96
hypothesis, 16, 18, 19

ideational concepts, 23, 78,
  110
identification with informants, 31, 75
illegal activities, 53
inactive tradition bearers,
  63n, 71, 150, 151
incentives (see *motivation*)
incidental collecting, 25
Indiana University, xv, 7n,
  172

induced context, 87-90, 151,
  153; limitations, 90
initial rapport, 59
insects, 34
interaction between participants, 73, 81, 92
interpretation, 2, 95-96, 105,
  134
interview data, kinds of, 104,
  106-108
interview methods, definition,
  77-78, 108-112
interviewing, 4, 12, 29, 31,
  70, 82, 83, 88, 89, 104-143,
  153, 155, 167
interviews, length of, 118-119
Introduction, 1-12
Ireland, field work in, 5n, 6n,
  23n, 33n, 151n, 154n, 156n,
  158n, 163
Isle of Man, 29n

Jackson, George P., 169-170
Jacobs, Melville, 8n
Jahoda, Marie, 76n, 82n,
  109n, 111n, 112n, 113n
Jamaica, 169
Jansen, William H., 62n, 71n,
  82n
jealousy, 74
Jewish collectors, 64
Johnson, James, viii
joining local organizations, 68
joking relationships, 70, 81
Jones, Louis C., 52n

Karpeles, Maud, 5n, 37n,
  39n, 44n, 167n, 168n

Keith, Alexander, 157n
Kinds of Folklore Data, 22-23
Kluckhohn, Clyde, 124n,
125n, 165n
Koch, William E., 10n
Korson, George, 122n
Krappe, Alexander H., 2n
Kroeber, A. L., xiv-xv, 2n

Labrador, 18
language, 11, 31, 38, 41, 52,
142, 171
Leach, MacEdward, xv, xvii,
4, 7, 8n, 18, 19, 169n, 172n
Leach, Maria, 1n
leads to informants, 39, 66,
67, 71, 144-145, 146, 148n,
151, 154
Leadbelly (see Ledbetter,
Huddie)
learning local occupations, 70
leave-time, 27, 28
Ledbetter, Huddie, 97, 122n
legends, 15m, 26
Legman, Gershon, 6n
levels in society, 49-50
libraries, 38, 40, 121
life histories, 121-122, 124,
125, 139, 163
limitations to methodology,
9-12, 175-176
Lindgren, E. J., 10n, 154n,
155n
liquor (see drinking with
informants)
literary aestheticians, 2n, 3, 4
literary folklorists, 2n, 4-5, 7,
14, 15
Lloyd, A. L., xvii

local assistants, 49-50, 56, 96,
101, 155, 171
local collecting projects, 25
local officials, 40, 55
Lomax, Alan, viii, xvii, xviii,
7, 102, 122n, 149n, 165n,
172, 173n
Lomax, John, 122n
Lones, T. E., 29n
Lowie, Robert H., 8n
lying by informants, 113-115

Mackenzie, W. Roy, 59n
magazines (see newspapers
and magazines)
Maine, 100
Malinowski, Bronislaw, 15n
manuals of folklore, 5
marbles, 87n, 90
mass communications media
(see communications
media)
Massachusetts, field work in,
xiv, 54
material culture, 11, 15n
Material Inducements,
166-172
matrix, 4, 125
McLendon, Altha L., 156n
McNeill, F. Marian, 29n, 69n
McPherson, J. M., 68n
Mead, Margaret, 93
meaning, 4, 6n, 85, 106-107,
140, 162, 166, 176
medical assistance, 65
memory distortion, 94, 142
memory retention, 94, 107,
119, 125, 142, 156
menstrual lore, 56

Merriam, Alan P., 42n
Michigan, 62n
milieu, 4
ministers, 40, 154
mnemonic devices, 89, 100,
    119
monetary payments, 150,
    166-169
Montgomerie, Norah and
    William, 158n
moonshining, 53
morality of role playing, 56-59
Morton, Jelly Roll, 122n
motivation, 30, 125, 160-173
Motivation and Remunera-
    tion of Informants, 160-173
mummers, 97
Murdock, G. P., 156n
Murray, M. A., 3
music, 5n
myths, 15n

Nadel, S. F., 114
nationalism, 53, 163
Negro informants, 54, 64, 98n,
    122n, 129n
New England, field work in,
    xvi, 18
Newfoundland, 172n
New York, field work in, xiv,
    74
newspapers and magazines,
    68, 144, 145-149
non-audience context, 43,
    128-129, 151, 153
non-directive interviews, 108-
    109, 110
non-financial assistance, 166,
    170-171

non-interview context,
    128-129
North America, 18
North Carolina, field work in,
    xiv, 53, 62, 64n, 161
Northrop, F. S. C., 16n, 17n,
    20n, 21n
notebooks, 41
note taking, 41-42, 79-80, 89,
    90, 94, 100, 119-121
Nova Scotia, 59n

Ó Súilleabháin, Seán, 5n, 6n,
    10, 23n, 151n, 156n, 163n,
    170n
obscene folklore, 45, 58-59,
    83, 115, 117, 128, 129-130,
    151, 153
observation, 11, 13, 29, 31,
    75, 77-103, 104, 113, 121,
    123, 127
observation methods,
    definition, 77
observation, recording of, 13,
    99-103
occupational folklore, 70
occupations of informants,
    37, 70, 118n, 122n
Opie, Iona and Peter, 158n
oral literature, 4, 8
ordering of materials, 123,
    136, 138, 141
Orkney and Shetland, 29n
Oster, Harry, xvii
over-motivation, 165
Ozarks, 52n, 59n, 60n

pads, 41-42
part-time collecting, x

participant, active, 78-80;
inactive, 78-80
participant observer, 78-80,
88, 94, 100
participation, 65-76, 164
participation fatigue, 31, 34,
75-76
participation, limits to, 72-76;
hazards of, 72-76
passive tradition bearers, 63n,
71
Paton, Cyril I., 29n
Paul, Benjamin D., 40, 47n,
51n, 53n, 54n, 72n, 73n,
78n, 91n, 164n
payment expectation, 169
Pennsylvania, University of,
xv, xvi, 7n
performance, classification, 82
performance style (see *style*)
personal history, 57, 106, 118,
121-127
personal services, 165, 170
personality, 9, 11, 14, 22, 28,
30, 33, 48, 59, 63, 75, 102,
108, 114, 125
Philadelphia, 129n
photographic equipment, 44,
97-99, 124-125, 163
Piddington, Ralph, 15n, 34n,
72n, 113n, 117n, 167n
poaching, 53
politics, 37
popular materials, 69, 135-136
popularists, 2n
practice with equipment,
42-43
predetermined conclusions,
19

pre-field preparations, 36-46,
49, 55
presumptive reasoning, 20
priests (see *ministers*)
privacy of informants, 72-73,
165
private family traditions, 71
problem analysis, 16, 20-22,
27, 33
problem revision, 27
problem solving, xiv, 16, 27,
32, 37, 76, 134, 135, 138,
140
problem statement, 16-20, 22,
27
Problem Statement and
Analysis, 13-26
processes, 8, 14, 23, 86, 100,
105, 162, 165, 166
professional collectors, viii,
4, 9, 14
professional folklorist,
definition, 3n, 5n, 9
professional performers, 95,
168
projective tests, 11, 124
protection of informants,
57-59
proverbs, 81, 94, 120
psychological gratification,
162-166
psychological tests (see
projective tests)
psychologists, xiii, 4
public entertainment, 69
pump-priming, 158-159

questionnaires, 5, 6, 10, 108,
139, 154-156

"quiet man" collector, ix

radio and television, 144, 149-150
Randolph, Vance, xvii, 52n, 59n, 60n, 148n
rapport, 30, 33, 40, 47-76, 84, 89, 109, 116, 117, 119, 131, 137, 148, 158, 164, 173
recipes, 68
recordings (see *tape recordings*)
regional collectors, 2n
re-interviewing, 113-114, 124
religion, 37, 62
remuneration, 150, 160-173
repertory, collector's, 44-45, 130-131, 150
repertory, informants, 60, 108, 112, 133, 134, 137-138, 158-159
repetitions of performance, 94-95, 138
residence (see *selection of residence*)
resident collector, ix, 10, 16, 148
rest periods, 34, 76
re-surveys, 18, 23, 29-30
review of data, 76, 97, 120
rhymes, 60, 94, 129-130, 147, 151, 153, 157
Richards, Audrey I., 7
Richmond, W. Edson, xv
riddles and riddling, 21, 44, 81, 87, 89, 94, 132, 147, 153, 157, 162
Ritchie, Jean, 33n, 97, 122n

rituals, 15n, 33, 69
road conditions, 37, 49
Roberts, Warren, xv
Rocky Mountains, 18
role changes, 56
role playing, ix, 51-59, 60, 65, 75, 76, 119
Rowe, John H., 100n
Russia, 122n
Rycroft, David, 44n

Sackett, S. J., 10n
safety copies, 43, 143
sampling, 32
Scarborough, Dorothy, 52n, 62n
school collecting projects, 151-154
School of Scottish Studies, xvi, 41n, 145
scientific inquiry, 6, 8, 13, 14, 15, 16, 17, 19, 27, 44, 58, 95, 132-133, 163, 165
Scotland, field work in, viii, xvi, 43, 53, 60, 62, 66, 67-69, 83, 85, 86, 89, 95, 112, 122n, 145, 153, 157-158, 163
secondary ethnocentrism, 31, 34
secret rites, 33, 83, 117
Seeger, Charles, xviii, 14n
selection of equipment, 42-43
selection of informants, 125-126
selection of materials, 133-138
selection of residence, 40, 48-51, 65
selective bias, 94, 95

self analysis, 34, 112, 169
self-consciousness, 80, 82, 85,
    102
Seligmann, C. G., 52n
sentiments expressed, 93
sensationalizing by reporters,
    147-148
separate recording of text and
    tune, 130
sex groups, 56, 72, 83, 128
sharing, 164-165, 171, 172-173
shorthand, 42, 119, 130
"shotgun" collecting, 25
shyness of informants, 128
simultaneous observations, 96
singing games, 21, 87n
situational familiarity, 85
"sizing-up" the collector, 59
social history, 37
social scientist, 2, 3, 13, 77
social visibility, 80
social workers, xiii
socializing with informants,
    12, 44-45, 59, 69, 70, 89,
    116, 131, 162, 164
sociologists, xiii, 4, 77
South America, 54
special pleaders, 2n
specialized knowledge,
    114-115, 125, 165
star informants, 71, 88, 98,
    121, 125, 153, 164
Stekert, Ellen, xvii
stimulants, 171-172
stranger value, 64, 71, 161,
    162
strangers, cautiousness to, 72,
    128
street singing, 98n

style, performance, 23, 45, 71,
    84, 85, 86, 87, 92, 98-99,
    101, 108
summer field trips, xiv, xv
"Sunday" collector, x
superstitions, 26, 56, 60, 66,
    68, 74, 132-133, 158
supplementary field methods,
    144-159
supplies, 34, 41-44, 45, 49,
    51, 65-66
survey projects, 24-25, 28,
    29-30, 37, 71, 134, 167
survivals, 17
Sweden, 154
synchronic comparison, 24

taboos, 39, 117
tall tales, 149n
tape recordings, 41, 42-44, 60,
    80, 89, 99-103, 119-120,
    129-130, 137-138, 142-143
taunts, 153
Taylor, Archer, xv, 157n
team collecting, 11, 25, 96
television (see radio and
    television)
temperature, 34
Thomas, Lowell, 149n
Thompson, Stith, 2n, 10n,
    14n, 53n, 154n, 157n, 163n
Thomson, William, viii
thumb-nail sketches, 121-122,
    124, 125, 139
time and duration of
    performance, 4, 92
time considerations, 21, 27-35,
    40, 46, 73-74, 103, 118,
    134, 136, 141

tiring informants, 61, 118
toasts, 26
tongue twisters, 153
topical works, 123-124, 125
tradition bearers, 4, 23, 26,
 55, 61, 106, 121, 122, 125,
 137, 153, 162
training, 2, 7, 11, 13, 14, 15,
 21, 22, 25, 32, 33, 47, 105,
 134, 165
transcriptions, 4, 41-42, 103,
 132-133, 142-143, 171
transient folklore, x, 63,
 160-162, 166
transmission, 107
transportation, 51, 65-66
traumatic disclosures, 34, 169
travel time, 32, 33, 37, 48
travelling collector, 63, 147,
 160-162
Trobriand Islands, 15n
Trout, Alan, 148n

unselfconsciousness, 85, 97,
 102

vacation collectors, 17, 24, 51
"vacuum cleaner" method,
 133-138
verbalization, 111-112, 125
vitality of tradition, 32, 41,
 175-176
von Sydow, C. W., 63n

water supplies, 34
wages, 166-169
weather conditions, 37, 43, 48
weather lore, 66, 81
Whitehead, A. N., x
wife as aid to collecting, 11,
 55-56, 66, 67, 68, 72, 96,
 101, 151
Wilgus, D. K., xviii
Wilson, Gordon, 148n
witchcraft, 68n, 115, 117, 147
women's folklore, 56, 67, 68
Wood, Ray, 148n
Wright, A. R., 29n
writer, role of, 54

Yanković, Ljubica S., 5